this porous fabric

Also by Ulrike Draesner

Poetry

hell & hörig: Gedichte 1995–2020 (2022)
doggerland (2021)
Nibelungen. Heimsuchung (2016)
subsong (2014)
berührte orte (2008)
kugelblitz (2005)
für die nacht geheuerte zellen (2001)
anis-o-trop (1997)
gedächtnisschleifen (1995)

Fiction

Schwitters (2020)
Kanalschwimmer (2019)
Sieben Sprünge vom Rand der Welt (2014)
Richtig liegen (2011, stories)
Vorliebe (2010)
Spiele (2005)
Hot Dogs (2004, stories)
Mitgift (2002)
Reisen unter den Augenlidern (1999, stories)
Lichtpause (1998)

Essays & Lectures

Grammatik der Gespenster: Frankfurter Poetikvorlesungen (2019)
Eine Frau wird älter (2018)
Die fünfte Dimension. Münchener Rede zur Poesie (2015)
Heimliche Helden (2013)
Schöne Frauen lesen (2007)
Zauber im Zoo (2007)

Travel

London (2016)
Mein Hiddensee (2015)

On Ulrike Draesner (in English)

Ulrike Draesner. A Companion. Edited by Karen Leeder and Lyn Marven. Berlin: Walter de Gruyter (2022).

Ulrike Draesner

this porous fabric

Selected Poems

translated from German by
Iain Galbraith

Shearsman Books

First published in the United Kingdom in 2022 by
Shearsman Books Ltd
PO Box 4239
Swindon
SN3 9FN

Shearsman Books Ltd Registered Office
30–31 St. James Place, Mangotsfield, Bristol BS16 9JB
(this address not for correspondence)

www.shearsman.com

ISBN 978-1-84861-785-8

The cover uses a still from a video treatment of the poem 'exit erdbeer-klee' (p. 220) by Stefan Harder, reproduced by kind permission of Stefan Harder:
https://www.youtube.com/watch?v=8zdovV_cko4

The translation of this work was supported by the German Translators' Fund under the *Neustart Kultur* programme, with resources provided by the Federal Government's Commissioner for Culture and Media.

Deutscher Übersetzerfonds

NEU START KULTUR

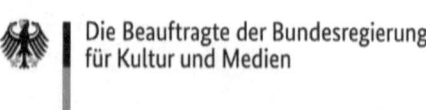

Die Beauftragte der Bundesregierung für Kultur und Medien

CONTENTS

kugelblitz (ball-lightning, 2005)

berührte orte (touched places, 2008)

subsong (subsong, 2014)

(UNCOLLECTED)

'from possible closeness': a translator's preface

Most of us learn to read the expression on a mother's face, the bounce of a ball, the changing colours of the sky. Translation of these phenomena into appropriate action rarely requires deep reflection. On the contrary, it appears instinctive; glancing at the clouds, we reach for an umbrella on our way out. To learn to read something is simultaneously, or perhaps necessarily, to find the key to its translation. That said, it may take a while for a translator to learn how to read a poem – months pass, years, even decades. There are times, too, when the luxury of a lengthy apprenticeship is denied, the attempt to read the poem cannot proceed, and hope of translation is abandoned. Conversely, and in the diehard spirit of the addict's dictum "Stopping is easy; it's staying stopped that is hard", a translation may triumphantly reach its completion – only to demand repeated redrafting ever after. If a poem or collection of poems is judged especially important, newer versions are sometimes undertaken by later generations of translators; as the world changes and we change with it new conditions permit different perspectives and open up works of art to compellingly fresh viewings. Perhaps it is wiser, then, to admit from the start the vanity of persuading anyone, least of all oneself, that finishing a translation can be anything more than a temporary measure. Poetry cannot be translated, the rumour-mongers will instruct you – and that is precisely where the fun starts, the translator will reply.

We may find that it is not only the finishing line but also translation's starting point that is difficult to establish. In one of her many essays on poetry and poetics, Ulrike Draesner, one of the preeminent poets of her generation, also an outstanding essayist and novelist, sees translating as an integral part of writing even before the poem is translated into a foreign language: "Literary writing means translating. From 'reality' into. From perception, from diffuseness into. From the semi- or non-linguistic into. From German into German".[1] Viewed thus, the route taken by a poem through various translation events and channels on its journey to the reader (whose own reading

[1] Ulrike Draesner. *Grammatik der Gespenster. Frankfurter Vorlesungen*. Ditzingen: Philipp Reclam jun. Verlag, 2018: 185.

is a form of translation, after all) appears more complex than we might otherwise have thought, and more continuous too: an ever-expanding fabric of metamorphic twists and turns woven between the Real, the "great outdoors", the "raw stuff of the world" or whatever you choose to call it, and any number of different readings in any number of languages. Language borders throughout this translatory terrain do not function as barriers. Porous, they crisscross the territories of our planetary semiosphere; they buffer, filter and form, encouraging transformation and the birth of new meaning.

As a German poet who has spent formative years of her life in England, Ulrike Draesner adds a further interlingual dimension to the genesis of her work when she avers that, for her, writing has meant developing ideas, images and voicings in one language within inward earshot of another: "I translate from German to German with the help of invisibly English structures, using them as a vantage point, as a breathing and thinking space which allows me to move freely in my writing language while at the same time viewing it from outside".[2] The technique, if that's what it is, may sound puzzling, but it is also more common than it sounds. Draesner may not be bilingual in any conventional sense of the term, and yet it is known that hundreds of writers worldwide live and write in more than one language, learning from an early age to analyse and shape one system of linguistic organization in view of another, their languages bouncing off one another within a mind rendered interlingually surveillant by cultural and historical circumstances.

One of the first poems of Ulrike Draesner's that I read was 'white horse' (the title is English in the German), included in her debut volume *gedächtnisschleifen* (memory loops, 1995). Since listening is no less a version of reading than following words on a page, I should add that my first acquaintance with 'white horse' was made at a poetry reading given by Ulrike Draesner on 27 October 1995 in the public library of the town where I live, shortly after her book had appeared. My reaction was one of excitement and immediate recognition. I was an insatiable poetry reader, and while closely following developments in British, Irish and U.S. poetry had found much to admire in newer German poetry too. In the 1980s I had read Volker Braun and Nicolas Born and was fascinated by the late Rolf Dieter Brinkmann's volume *Westwärts 1&2*, but also younger poets such as Uwe Kolbe, Werner Söllner and Durs Grünbein.

---

[2] ibid, 185.

In the early 1990s it was work by Dieter M. Gräf, Gerhard Falkner, Jürgen Becker, Peter Waterhouse, Marcel Beyer and Thomas Kling that excited me, but also the younger poets from the GDR such as Bert Papenfuß-Gorek, Kerstin Hensel, Sascha Anderson, Stefan Döring and Rainer Schedlinski, all of whom I had begun to read in the late 1980s. Nonetheless I had not come across anything like Draesner's work in German before, and I straightaway felt close to its grammar and texture. A glance at the names I have mentioned above reveals that there were very few female poets on my reading list, and that absence reflected the undeniably male German poetry scene at the time. Much has changed; some twenty-five years later I shall venture to claim that most of the best poetry published in German today is by women. In retrospect I can see that what I had admired in Ulrike Draesner's work, but had few words for then, was its integration of phantom and sensory perception, its exploration of the involuntary loops of memory, its head-on rushes and equally impulsive recoils into silence, its tentative reflection, its layering and deconstruction, all strangely recognizable and thrillingly unexpected as composed speech:

> with my nail
> i hatch (such as fingers can)
> the long mouth the nostrils soft
> all conjured up in stone, the rock
> always muter than you think, the eye
> close in seeing no lines at all
> only this blanched body

It was not just that the poems I listened to that evening had found an echo in my own sensibility, it was that they also felt more *real* than the "univocal, more or less plainspoken, short narrative often culminating in a sort of epiphany", as Rae Armantrout, in an essay published in 1992, had recently described what she called the "conventional or mainstream poem".[3] I was not quite prey to the rivalrous enmity that sometimes accompanies envy, but I did desire to make these poems my own in whatever way I could, to work through them for what had inspired me, for the sense of an opening that seemed to lead to a more intensely present and barer ("blanched", perhaps) version of my own

[3] Rae Armantrout. 'Feminist Poetics and the Meaning of Clarity.' *Sagetrieb* 11.3 (Winter 1992): 7-16.

thoughts and sensations – and translation seemed the obvious next step. Within a month of that first encounter I had produced a first English version of 'white horse'. Since then the translation has been revised again and again, with the most recent change made only a few months ago, more than twenty-five years after my first reading.

The closing lines of the poem seem to me now to capture something of that initial, engrossed listening and recognition, although they first of all speak of emerging consciousness in the "i" of the poem, who has come straight from a reading too, albeit a "reading" of what I imagine to be the Uffington White Horse, a prehistoric geoglyph in the Berkshire Downs and, at some 3,000 years old, the most ancient of several such chalk figures in the British Isles:

> down in the pub THEY'RE
> CHALKING UP THE DEBTS this ever open
> mazy chalk screeching into the slate
> which i – having sucked in through nostrils
> a cantering long-necked rock – know
> from where? from possible closeness
> from layers of it

One thing that strikes me about 'white horse' and which is typical enough of the author's work to deserve attention here, is its emphasis on the body as the receptor and fount of the engagement that informs both experience and knowledge as well as the writing process itself: in other words, as the locus of that barely fathomable sentience which generates the consistency and projection of the text as well as our ability to read it. As readers we are carried along (just as we are invited to loop and return) by the poem's restlessly inquisitive diction and the probing inclination of its lines: which is also to say that we are guided by breathing, voicing and rhythm, as well as by aural and visual response, by the patterns of sound-making and imaging that provoke our interactions with the writing ("into my gradually sliced / body memory flamed / scratchings"). The poem seems to be telling us that the body, and consequently the body's poetic utterance, is both the repository and oracle of our individual and collective experience.

Writing from and to the body is also the context within which we should understand Draesner's initially unaccustomed manner of handling punctuation and capitalization, which she perceives as significant organizers of the printed surface of texts. German conventionally prescribes commas to indicate the beginning of subordinate clauses, for example, and capitalizes the first letter of nouns. For Draesner, the former can act as an arbitrary, indeed counterproductive signal to the reader's breathing, interfering with the intended voicing patterns of the poem, while mandatory and therefore indiscriminate capitalization can convey a weighting upon nouns that overstates their relative importance in a phrase or sentence. Conversely, the omission of capitals, commas and other punctuation where these do not fulfil a specified meaningful function in the poem can facilitate profitable ambiguity, in part through what one might call synergetic syntax (e.g. words or phrases shared by contiguous sentences to the effect that more than two possible sentences emerge), while at the same time providing new means to pace the reading. Sound sequencing (rhyme, assonance etc.) may then emerge more clearly as the source of navigation and connectivity it intends to be; contrarily, the reader's progress, surprised by apparent non-sequiturs that appear to hinder the delivery of meaning, may slow to a stutter (a significant word in Draesner's poetics), while the eye searches for the connective tissue of syntax and – like the "eye" or "i" in 'white horse' – "constructs what it sees".

Seen in this way, the composed scriptural surface belongs to the body of the poem in the same way ideas, traditional forms and rhyme do; it is in fact the interfacial membrane between breathing and meaning. It cannot therefore be left to the masters of linguistic convention (ultimately, as far as the German language is concerned, the intermittent reforming zeal of language committees and conferences set up by ministries of education in Germany, Austria, Liechtenstein and Switzerland) or to the arbiters of good taste (again, in German, the academies, learned councils and societies, prescriptive style guides and dictionaries like the famous *Duden*) to decide what can or cannot be part of a poem. The English language does not have the same range of watchful institutions, and yet, in the UK as in the US, whether as translator or author, one's writing may collide with the impositions of rigorous "house style", and there are still editors who consider alpha-numeric variants, even sometimes the use of lower case, to be a wilful attack on the common reader's alleged right to communicative clarity.

Aside from the fact of poetry's ancestral proximity to the arts of song and dance in which the body plays such an obvious role, there is nonetheless something like common sense in focussing on the body when we speak of poetry. "What is a lyric poem", the poet Charles Simic asks, "but the recreation of the experience of Being".[4] And what are the peculiarities of such sentience – or "qualia", as neuroscientists and modern philosophers have called the illusive "feel" of conscious being – without the transmissions of our sensory cortices. Metrical rhythms and their aberrations can affect our heartbeat, while the lines and their relative length can visualize the changes and projection of our breathing and regulate the flow of reading. Ulrike Draesner has repeatedly accentuated the interaction between the outer world and the inner world of the body in essays and interviews reflecting on her own poetry or that of other poets.[5] In an interview from 2005 she describes how the emergent poem integrates diverse stimuli in the course of an attentively reflective process of composition, revealing that most Romantic of organs, the heart, to be quite literally, indeed physiologically, at the centre of her poetic workspace:

> The real human body lends corporeity to writing – it gives it its voice – so that the poem arises in the light of that body, is transported from one body to others. At the same time, for me, writing a poem too is always bound up with bodily experience in which breath and pulse – which might be one's own heartbeat or could be the impulse occasioned by a word – determine the making of a poem. […] The pulse, initiated by an impulse sent through the body by the cardiac muscle, can be read at the wrist, a typical interface between what we think of as the interior or inner world of the body and the outside world. […] An impulse is something that comes from outside. It might be a ball banging into another ball, for instance, or something banging into me, changing the direction of my thoughts or the way I express myself. That fairly exactly describes my experience of writing a poem. There's the pulse and there's an impulse;

[4] Charles Simic. *The Life of Images. Selected Prose.* New York: HarperCollins Publishers, 2015: 12.

[5] Poets Ulrike Draesner has mentioned as influential on her work at various times include the 20th-century Austrian writer Ingeborg Bachmann, the Viennese poets Friederike Mayröcker and Reinhard Priessnitz, the language archaeologist and performative ecstatic Thomas Kling, the great German 19th-century poet Annette von Droste-Hülshoff (1797–1848) and Draesner's Canadian contemporary Karen Solie, as well as those she has translated into German, such as Louise Glück, Gertrude Stein or Michèle Métail.

> when they meet, each changes the other. [T]he impulse can also be language; a quotation from a 200-year old poem darting through my mind. At the same time this impulse encounters my pulse, the heartbeat of the person I happen to be at that moment, with my feelings, the force of my thoughts ... [A]nd if the moment is propitious ... something happens, something new arrives, which could be a poem.[6]

However, the centrality of the body in Ulrike Draesner's work does not halt at its functional contribution to poem-making. She has also indicated that poetry to her is a site of discovery and tentative experimental practices, and while her writing (whether in novels or poetry) often reflects an interest in science in general, whether in zoology, climate science, physics, molecular biology, linguistics or cybernetics, it has often also been the (female) body with which her poems have engaged.

For Ulrike Draesner poetry does not primarily serve to "give expression to subjective sensibilities", whether these be "beautiful" or less so. Instead, she sees poetry as a "form of research" into our "mentality", as language-work that attempts to investigate the "human tissue" of our "feelings, thoughts and actions" or, as she also describes it, "the way we are put together".[7] Experimental practice of this kind can have its place in a love poem, a poem about a bird, a walk on the beach or the use of an escalator, and it can be found in her earliest work, in the poems included in the present volume from *memory loops* (*gedächtnisschleifen*), for example, in 'secretion', 'hermaphrodite proem' or 'north room', also in 'shingles' or 'seedbed (autopilot IV)'. In the last of these the "sensibilities" under observation are ostensibly those of someone who has undergone a heart transplant and is now standing at the grave of the person whose heart "she" carries in her breast. A "dead man" has "taken" in her body and made of her a "seedbed". Which perplexing state of affairs leads to an obvious question: which of them, if either, is speaking? And who, for that matter, is dead? Are we hearing the ruminations and private confessions of a lyrical "I", and if so, who or what is that? What kind of "human tissue" is he, she or it made

[6] 'Ulrike Draesner im Gespräch mit Christian Schlösser.' *Deutsche Bücher. Forum für Literatur* 35.4 (2005): 269-271.

[7] 'Bewegung in Sprache. Ulrike Draesner im Gespräch mit Rolf Bernhard Essig'. *neue deutsche literatur* 51:6 (2003): 52.

of? This is a graveside address that inevitably questions the reliability of the speaker; indeed the speaking subject might be considered composite or various, involving different people and including a body part (a speech from the heart, only whose?). It is as if Draesner's first task on entering the poetry scene is to bury any remaining traditional assumption about the "lyrical I", at the same time making us witness to the rich quandary its decease has left behind. It is true that the sciences of the body – organ transplantation, reproductive medicine, genetics and cloning, neurobiology, psychology and other disciplines have haunted Ulrike Draesner's poems from the start, but it is equally the case that the presence of such matter, as even my succinct reading of 'seedbed (autopilot IV)' may suggest, is not intended to further our STEM-field education.

Poem sequences play an important role in Draesner's work. These may consist of as few as two poems, but the longer sequences allow the poet to pursue more extensive, processual developments as well as varying perspectives and structural patterns. One such sequence in the present selection is the explorative 'bluish sphinx / (cloud', from Draesner's second major volume *für die nacht geheuerte zellen* (*cells hired for the night*, 2001). The sequence consists of 10 poems[8] of varying length centring around the experience of a "missed abortion" (one of the poems uses this term in English), also known as a missed or "silent" miscarriage: in other words a non-elective abortion in which the embryo or foetus has died but has not left the uterus. In some cases where the miscarriage has not completed, a doctor may recommend dilation of the cervix and curettage (scraping) of the uterus or vacuum aspiration (suction). As this description already suggests, a woman's experience of exposure to invasive medical technology links all 10 poems of the sequence. While it is obviously necessary for a translator who is unacquainted with the medical details to undertake background research, and while the poems present a subjective response to the alienating environments and overwhelming procedures of machine medicine and healthcare, it is not only these aspects of the experience that will detain the reader. For me, at least, this powerful sequence is memorable first and foremost as a

[8] Perhaps there are more, with the sequence even leaping between poems in different volumes: compare for example the imagery in the second half of 'op' in this sequence with that of the poem 'hiddensee, south beach, the beckoning bay', in the 2005 collection *ball-lightning*, and included in the present volume, or, available in German only, with her memoir of the Baltic island Hiddensee, *Mein Hiddensee* (2015), pp. 96-8.

moving encounter with a vulnerable female speaker's trauma and grief at the loss of a desired child, a crisis of mind and body followed into the tiniest fragments and structures of her conscious experience. At the same time, however, and in the light of Ulrike Draesner's poetry as a whole, there is another aspect of the sequence to which I should like to call the reader's attention.

By the time we read the first poem, with its own title 'song in the belly', the overall title of the sequence has already handed us an enigma: 'bluish sphinx / (cloud'.[9] First of all we may wonder what the "sphinx" is, and why it is "bluish" (not even blue), but then what is meant by the "(cloud" with its unclosed bracket? The sphinx has lost no time in setting us riddles to solve, it would seem, drawing us into its intriguing domain even before we reach a bracket 16 lines later, which closes behind the question we have just asked: "but what is meant by / 'cloud')". Whether or not the poem provides an answer to this question (without a question mark) is something every reader may answer differently. But what immediately follows the cloud could at least be a pointer: "tiny root, you". The existence of a "you" inevitably suggests an "i", who is presumably the speaker of the poem, or at least of these lines. The "root" appears to reference the embryo, but perhaps something else has taken root too. The embryo is dead, but with this address we have a new, vital pronoun, "you", and with it a new entity in the text, a companion figure. That is almost as much as I can say about it: a ghostly presence that is from now on a shape-shifting figure in the text and, albeit as a shadow, or as a negative perhaps, grows like any child or companionship might. Importantly, the lonely or at least single "i" itself has metamorphised into a different kind of being: a heterocentric subject:[10] later in the sequence the pronominal "i" alternates with a "we". Perhaps we can say that the "cloud" foreshadows the dialogical

---

[9] The German title 'bläuliche sphinx (wolke', taken from Ulrike Draesner's forthcoming selected poems in German, *hell & hörig* (Penguin, 2022), differs from the original title of the sequence in *für die nacht geheuerte zellen* (2001), which is 'bläuliche sphinx / (metall)'; "metall" heads a section of the 2001 volume, with other section titles also representing traditional acupuncture elements: wood, fire, earth, water.

[10] I adapt the term 'heterocentric', the opposite of egocentric, from its use by John MacMurray, for whom the 'personal' contained centres outside the self. "The personal is constituted by personal relatedness. The unit of the personal is not the 'I', but the 'You and I'", and: "'I' exist only as one element in the complex 'You and I'". *Persons in Relation*, London: Faber, 1961: 24.

subject *in statu nascendi*, a personal relatedness, the speaker as emergent community. What may at first have seemed like a splitting of the subject, a quasi-schizoid fragmentation localised in this sequence and born of grief, is established here (if it had not already been introduced in earlier poems) as Ulrike Draesner's characteristic lyrical subject: multi-centric, diverse, grammatical, all-inclusive.

Above I used the term "lyrical subject" instead of the more common "lyrical I", because the grammatical subject need be neither a first person singular nor human; it can be single, multiple, composite, animate or inanimate. But if it speaks, should we nevertheless describe it as a first person, an ego, even when the text uses third person pronouns or indeed no pronoun at all? Draesner confirms that the "I" itself really is no more than a pronoun, a linguistic position, a "placeholder telling us: here is a perceiving entity". A communicative ghost, then, but with none of the fullness of a fictional or biographical figure or character:

> If we think of poetry as a route the voice takes as it leaves the body in language, whence it proceeds to inhabit other bodies, it immediately becomes clear why it makes such an excellently ghostly art form. Its famous "lyrical I" may be a useful academic invention, but it is usually a fairly lightsome, if not flighty figure. Often enough, with no more presence than a pronoun, it isn't a figure at all. Perception without an ego, without the whole body, without a history – that is enough for poetry. In what appears to be the most natural manner, the grass itself may speak directly, or a drop of water, or a swarm. Or one's own body, like at the end of 'what is poetry?', the final poem in my collection *subsong*.[11]

In Ulrike Draesner's volume *subsong* (2014) language invents itself anew as the poems emerge, their shifting voices stemming from the poems' personae, from a hare in its form, a small child who cannot yet mouth certain sounds, the Beatles' songs in homophonic German versions, copulating wasps, a mother, a hen blackbird, or a snipe ("tick-a tick/keek-keek-keek") in its biotope ("silt-grey/ slate-grey: sky-/strapped gleaming scurf-/stump") which merges into a passing woman. If the "lyrical I" is no more than a ghost, a voluble

[11] Ulrike Draesner. *Grammatik der Gespenster. Frankfurter Vorlesungen*: 127.

space, what or who is it then that speaks? Not the author, surely, not even language, as Heidegger famously posited ("Die Sprache spricht": language speaks). It is of course the poem that speaks, an entity separate from its author and separate too from any of its different individual pronouns, a poem composed not only in German within earshot of English, but in all the tongues it acquires: porous shrub, child, snipe, cyberjewel, pronounless you-and-me. Poems are "gloves with a thousand fingers", Ulrike Draesner once wrote, "and a thousand and one loopholes".

Wiesbaden,
20th October 2021

Acknowledgements

I should like to thank the editors of the following books and journals where some of the translations initially appeared: *After Brecht.* Edited by Karen Leeder. Manchester: Carcanet Press (2006), *Agni, Atlanta Review, The Café Review, Manoa. A Pacific Journal of International Literature, Modern Poetry in Translation, New European Poets.* Edited by Wayne Miller and Kevin Prufer. Graywolf Press (2008), *Poetry Review* and *Ulrike Draesner. A Companion.* Edited by Karen Leeder and Lyn Marven. Berlin: Walter de Gruyter (2022). I am also indebted to the Rotterdam International Poetry Festival and Poetry International Festival (Southbank Centre, London), as well as to New College, Oxford's 'Leaping from the Edge of the World', a symposium on the work of Ulrike Draesner, each of which commissioned translations of a number of the poems.

gedächtnisschleifen

1995

memory loops

1995

im stroh

hockten im stroh wie in den
innersten ängsten, auf den
katzenköpfen hallte der
einspänner, milchabfuhr.
zu molke geschlagen hüteten
wir die phantasie, unten
suchte uns einer, landverschickung
von kriegskindern, nachtblinden
tagträumern, während wir uns
noch einmal umhalsten, bruder
um jeden sinn uns brachten
hersagend den stand der
dinge, voreinander, vor
den leichen im stroh.

in the straw

we hunkered down in the straw
as if amidst inmost fears while
the horse and cart came clanging
over the cobbles to fetch the milk.
beaten to whey we tended
the fantasy someone below
was looking for us, evacuation
of war-kids, moon-blind
day-dreamers, and we hugged
each other again, brother
robbing each other of rhyme
and reason, intoning the state of
things, face to face, in the
face of the corpses in the straw.

sekret

heimlich lohender hinter schwarzen ästen
wintermorgen klebte an doppelten scheiben
völlig keimfrei die ärzte sagten ›drüsen‹
betasteten nacheinander den stoffwechsel
kein grund zur sorge ein salzeinlauf löst
die verklemmung ich kam auf die schüssel
im gesicht wiederholte sich schließmuskelglätte
mein stockendes sprechen – da habe ich plötzlich
auf dem pythiastuhl habe kein wort mehr heraus-
bringen, plötzlich den mund nicht bewegen können
mir war, ich würde nie mehr, solche kehlenangst
schnürte mir den speichel, darunter meine zuckenden
rasenden muskeln, jemand sagte: vielleicht
drüsenpressen, unerklärlicher eiweißausfluss, alle
instrumente kreiseln ja, da hob ich mich schon
nicht mehr ab von dem wintermorgen dem weiß
dem grau hob mich nicht mehr vor dem hintergrund
als eigenfigur heraus kleine rauchwölkchen
geheime sekrete schwebten mir aus allen
schädelöffnungen dampften zu den ohren
nasenlöchern augen den ja wieder geöffneten
fontanellen heraus – betäubende buchstabentiere

vergleiche holzschnitt um 1450
über hautgrund abgebildetes entweichen
sogenanntes schönes durcheinander-
kriechen von seelen

secretion

secretly blazing behind black branches
a winter's morning clung to double panes
wholly aseptic the doctors said "glands"
in succession palpating my metabolism
no cause for worry a saline enema will
undo the deadlock i was put on the pan
levelling of the facial sphincter recurred
my speech faltered – and then suddenly
on the seat of pythia could not speak
not a word could not move my mouth
felt i'd never again, such pharyngeal anxiety
choking my saliva, below which my twitching
raging muscles, someone said: possibly
glandular pressure, inexplicable protein discharge
all the dials were spinning, by now i no longer
stood out from the winter's morning white
and grey no longer stuck out as a separate
figure against the background tiny smoke-
clouds secret secretions fumed from my
every cranial orifice wafted from ears
nostrils eyes my, yes, reopened
fontanelles – numbing animal letters

compare woodcut ca. 1450
depicted on a skin background the escape
the so-called beautiful inter-
seething of souls

gottesanbeterin, glühend

erstes ćevapčići – gedächtnis
von zikaden bei zedern und pinien
abendtaumelnde eintagsfliege, am fleisch,
als das erste essen serviert wird, erstes meer
wird sie die glühendste, die gottesanbeterin: cara
carissima, alle zukunftsbriefe
schriften nach innen, das reiben der
fühler ein zeichen, am meer deuten
die herrschenden götter jede bewegung,
das zirpen und zucken, falten der
beine, weil die fliegen nur einen
tag leben, weil das nicht zu verstehen
nicht ist, was es heißt, dass das bettier
sein paarungsfleisch frisst, sie, cara,
sechs jahre, am ersten meer, schwören,
beißen, schlingen munden von selbst, hinauf
bei pinien, zedern, zikaden
hinab werden die finger geübt, was
nicht zu verstehen ist, während sie (innerer brief),
von nirgendwoher nirgendwohin nabelgeschnürt
in die eintagsfliegenordnung, eine frau wird,
vorm gefalteten fühler der anbeterin, während
sie sich mit gabel und messer erstes
ćevapčići, gedächtnis, in den mund kreuzt
das glühende hackstück auf ex.

praying mantis, glowing

first ćevapčići – memory
of cicadas with cedars and pines
tumbling evening dayfly, on the meat
as the first meal is served, first sea
she will glow most, the praying mantis: cara
carissima, in all future-letters
inward writings, its rubbing of
forelegs a sign, the gods holding sway
divining every stir of the sea
every churr and twitch, and folding
of legs, because flies live only
for a day, because it can't be understood
not what it means when the praying creature
devours its mating flesh, she, cara
six years old by her first sea, vowing
biting, gobbling herself, savouring, up there
with pines cedars cicadas
below her fingers learning, not
to be understood, while she (inward letter)
from one no-place to another, umbilically tied
to the order of dayflies, becomes a woman
before the folded feeler of the adorer, while
she with knife and fork crosses in her
mouth first ćevapčići, memory, the
glowing meat-chunk, death

hermaphroditisches proëm

hermaphrodit nacktkühle marmor-
gestalt zwischen dem blattwerk verdecktes
von schatten wie fingern kastaniengeblüt
in weiß, ich begreife den langgezogenen leib
im gestriemten becken treibt die sichel
des mondes, der nabel, ich sehe wie mir
die blanke aufwölbung des bauches mir hermes
sprecher der liebe, gleitender bote, wie mir
die sehende hand, des arztes äskulap, hermaß
den inneren bauchraum, tastete die redselige
örtlichkeit blutwallung beinahe nicht zu orten
die beine entlaufen in den zärtlichen fischschwanz
beginnen die menschen hermetisch von alters her
daumengroß der kopf auf dem bild-schirm
ein schatten zum leben gerissene
zwitterform, däumling
mein flimmerndes kind

hermaphrodite proem

coolly-naked marble hermaphrodite
figure among the leafage hidden
by fingery shadows a chestnut-kindred
in white, i take in the elongate body
adrift in the striate pelvis the crescent
moon, the navel, see the bare bulge
of my belly, how hermes speaker of love
gliding messenger, how the seeing hand
doctor asclepius's measured my
ventral interior touched the voluble
locus in quo, a blood-surge barely palpable
the legs running to that endearing fishtail
humans were hermetic from the first
the thumb-sized head on the image-screen
a shadow, androgynous form
wrenched into life, thumbling
my shimmering child

nordzimmer I

im nordzimmer
in der fensterbank sitzend
des nordzimmers vor rechteckig
ausgeschnittenen lindenbaumfächern
honigfarbener fernsehturm (dämmerungsspitze)
langsam blinkend durch laub die satellitenschüssel
gegenüber weiß wie das weiche gewebe der
wünsche nach oben gebogen auffangschale
eines vorsichtigen beklopfens aus der luft
ständige flug- vogel- und knochengeräusche
einer gesteigerten eintragskunst in die gerasterte
wölbung von innen meiner schädelschüssel vielleicht
nervenschnee der wahre kunsttrieb wo sich augenhöhlen
sich neu aushöhlen etwas ständigsickernd weiches
an der gelierenden fontanelle (knochenbeugung)
heraus von weichem durch schädel hinein
durch schädel zu weichem sich zeilendes
vernetzungswerk (dritte pupille): schon
pulsend aus nervengitter vom
inneren ossarium: musendiktat
funkend / ohne *mus-*
ter : einen
kuss schnee
weißen kuss
durchs ge
stöber

north room I

in the north room
sitting in the window seat
of the north room in front of linden
tree-fans cut into oblongs
the honey-coloured television tower (twilight point)
slowly blinking through leaves the satellite dishes
opposite white as the soft tissue of
wishes upward-curved a bowl receiving
a tentative tip-tap from the air
the incessant sound of aircraft bird and bone sounds
of a heightened art of inscription into the rastered
vault from within of my cranial dish perhaps
neural snow the true artistic impulse where eye-sockets
hollow themselves out anew a softness at the jelling
fontanelle (bone flexion) continually seeping
from softness outward via the cranium inwards
via the cranium to softness a meshwork
line-linking (a third pupil): pulsing
now from the neural grid of the
inner ossuary: dictated by the muse
sparking / without *pat-*
tern : a
kiss a snow
white kiss
through the flu-
rry

nordzimmer II

im nordzimmer
in der fensterbank sitzend
des nordzimmers vor rechteckig
ausgeschnittenen lindenbaumfächern
honigfarbener fernsehturm (dämmerungsspitze)
langsam blinkend durch laub die satellitenschüssel
gegenüber weiß wie das weiche gewebe der
wünsche nach oben gebogen auffangschale
eines vorsichtigen beklopfens aus der luft
vielleicht gedanken oder

du aus allen himmeln du
verstreut in alle himmelsrichtungen
ich knie im fenster am nomadenteppich
betasten meine haarspitzen unlesbare muster ich
knie im betgewand auf meinen wanderschuhen sind
fünf weiße hundepfoten erschienen (versunken)
türkische vokale örtülmüs ürkek özlem
so zirpt das dunkle rot die linke brustspitze
wiedergesehen im webmuster das mich als
auge anblickt krümmt mich zum stirnfall
stirnkuss auf den flugteppich schüttelt mich
lindentrommeln infamer duft in den
griff einer schleunigen liebe

north room II

in the north room
sitting in the window seat
of the north room in front of linden
tree-fans cut into oblongs
the honey-coloured television tower (twilight point)
slowly blinking through leaves the satellite dishes
opposite white as the soft tissue of
wishes upward-curved a bowl receiving
a tentative tip-tap from the air
thoughts perhaps or

you fallen from heaven you
scattered to the four winds
i kneel in the window hair ends
touching illegible patterns on the nomad rug i'm
in a prayer robe kneeling, five white dog's paws
have appeared on my walking boots (absorbed)
turkish vowels örtülmüs ürkek özlem
thus chirps the dark red the tip of my left breast
seen again in the weaving pattern looking at me
like an eye bending me into a brow-fall
brow-kiss rocking me on the flying carpet
a linden drumming shameful fragrance into
the grasp of a hurried love

haare, küssend

beredter holunder dieser
vielzungige holunder mein begieriger
liebeshunger wie ich mit allen haarsträhnen
wärmste befederung oder umarmung dich umfasste von
der seite dir um den nacken die wangen strich mit wehenden
haaren meine weißen tastenden dolden phantasiezungen
um dich schlang dass du ganz geflochten

stocktest,

als du gingst,
mitten im satz, dich
zu mir neigtest, bis meine lippen
auf deiner wange streiften meine lippen
bartstoppeln spürten einen tastenden augenblick
deine gefiederte antwort voraus: aufrauschen und vorübergehn

hair, kissing

eloquent elder bush this
many-tongued elder my greedy
hunger for love the way with warmest feathering
or embracing with all the coils of my hair I clasped you
from the side stroking your nape your cheeks with flowing
hair my probing white umbels my fantasy tongues
entwining you so that completely entangled you

faltered

as you left,
in mid-sentence,
leant over me till my lips
brushed against your cheek my lips
felt your bristles a fumbling moment long
ahead of your feathered response: hackles up and away

dein kommen war in teilen,
die bald überwogen, ein gehen,
weil das kommen, deines, nur einen
teil seiner selbst, seiner bedeutung
hatte, dieses, von vornherein, kommen
in teilen, was aber nicht zu erkennen war,
nicht gleich, nicht für mich,

doch kam, als du kamst, nur ein teil
deiner selbst, weil es von vornherein
teil der bedeutung deines kommens
war, was heißt, daß dieses in
geteilten teilen kommen teil
der bedeutung dessen war, dass
du kamst und wieder gingst,
weil die bedeutung deines kommens
von anfang an ungeteilt war, nämlich
dieses, dein gehen, in teilen.

your coming was in parts
that soon tipped the balance, a going,
because this coming, yours, was only
a part of itself, of its meaning,
which was, from the first, a coming
in parts, though this was not apparent,
not at once, not to me

but what came, when you came, was only a part
of yourself, because it had from the first
been a part of the meaning of your coming,
which is to say that this
coming in part of parts was part
of the meaning of the fact
that you came and then went again,
because the meaning of your coming
was from the first clear in every part,
namely this: your going, in parts.

white horse

felsbild white horse
das auge setzt was es sieht
nur aus der ferne zusammen
die pupillen schlitzt jedem
das englische gegenlicht
als wir, busschwall, auf das bild
zugehen, kreide, mein erlöschendes
gesicht, mit dem nagel schraffiere
ich nach (was man mit fingern)
das lange maul, die weichen nüstern
alles hochgesprochener stein, der fels
ist immer stummer als man denkt, das auge
sieht aus der nähe überhaupt keine linien
nur diesen blanchierten körper, hier
wächst nichts mehr, hier kann keiner
mehr anwachsen, nie mehr, linien, ritzen
während du da warst : wir, sah ich
nichts, in meinen allmählich tranchierten
körper die einflammende erinnerung
ritzende sind's, meine haut, tiefritzende
ritzen
            unten, im pub, SCHREIBEN SIE
DIE SCHULDEN AN diese immer offene
wirre kreide kreischend in den schiefer
was ich – durch nüstern gesogen ein
trabender langhalsiger fels – weiß
von wo? von möglicher nähe
von schichten davon

white horse

white horse done in rock
the eye constructs what it sees
only from afar
the english contre-jour
slitting our pupils
as we, surge from a bus, head
for the image, chalk, my fading
face, with my nail
i hatch (such as fingers can)
the long mouth the nostrils soft
all conjured up in stone, the rock
always muter than you think, the eye
close in seeing no lines at all
only this blanched body, here
nothing more will grow, here no body
can take root, not ever, lines, scratches
while you were here : we, i saw
nothing, into my gradually sliced
body memory flamed
scratchings, these are, my skin, deep-scratching
scratches
                down in the pub THEY'RE
CHALKING UP THE DEBTS this ever open
mazy chalk screeching into the slate
which i – having sucked in through nostrils
a cantering long-necked rock – know
from where? from possible closeness
from layers of it

gürtelrose

es ist vorbei. aus und vergessen.
was zwischen uns war. sagst du.
gehst gegen das sprechen. erinnern.
gegen mich. wortlos. auf fahrt.
doch was nicht sein darf. ist doch.
wie der wind. den erst keiner sieht.
als schaum. auf der welle.
als beugung. im baum.

wo du auch bist, ist vorbei
wie du dich auch kennst, vergessen
dein innerer mensch klammert
(sehnsucht), langsam und schweigend, wo
alle richtungen verstellt sind, einen gürtel
(rettungssprache) von innen nach außen
dir durch, aus dem in dich rinnenden
trennungsschweiß, da dreht der wind
sich aus sich selbst, greift in die nerven
von innen, flammend, am körper, dir
eine schlagende sprache, dass die knoten
schäumen und glühen, dein gesamtes hautgewand
redeentzündet, wellt, dehnt sich mir entgegen
in allen fasern, in all deinen fibern
dass jeder sieht: der wind ist am sturm
nicht der sturm, aber seine zunge
und dein körper, beredt
gehört mir.

shingles

it's over. done and dusted.
whatever was between us. you say.
you're against talking. remembering.
against me. wordless. in a temper.
but what cannot be. in fact is.
like wind. that no one sees at first.
as foam. on the wave.
as bending. in a tree.

wherever you are is over
however you saw yourself forgotten
your inner being clamps
slowly and silently (yearning), all
routes being blocked – a girdle
(rescuing tongue) through yourself from within
to without, it's made of the separation sweat
flowing into you, it's the wind twisting
out of itself, clawing at nerves
from within, flaming, a language
that batters your body so that blisters
foam and glow, the entire robe of your skin
inflamed with speech, undulating, straining
toward me in all its fibres and filaments
so that all may see: the wind
of the storm is not the storm but its tongue,
and your body, eloquent
belongs to me.

pflanzstätte (autopilot IV)

zitternder körper, verpflanzungsgebiet – im
zitternden körper, meinem, schlägt dieses herz
fremdgänger, als ich am grab stehe (auslöser)
zitternd über dem toten, über den erdpflanzen
(angegangen), ein losgelöstes augenflattern
so heftig flimmern diese herzwände
erkennen den ort wieder (ein segen die
moderne medizin), unten das bodyasyl
armenhaus, erkennen sie wieder, davon
hat keiner gesprochen, von diesen verkettungen
diesem herzreden, nadelspitzer elektrosturm
in meiner brust (pflanzstätte) angegangen
ein toter, die grablege reicht was
hinüber ein klammern reicht aus dem grab
ein restleben (rhythmuserinnerung), nichts messbares
diese plötzliche geschwindigkeitsneigung, meine
mir einflüsternder dämon, dolmetsch
eines anderen lebens, haltlos, kammernzuckend
als ich weine an diesem grab
da werde ich (herzmade) zum langsam
zernagten, von innen
wirt eines toten

seedbed (autopilot IV)

trembling body, transplant zone – in the
trembling body, mine, this heart is beating
a stray, while at the grave (prime mover)
i tremble over the dead man over soil plants
(taking), eyes flicker of their own accord
so fiercely fluttering these heart's walls
recognize the place (such a blessing
modern medicine), below the body's asylum
a poor house, recognize them too but
nobody told me of this, this interlinking
this heart-chatter, the needle-sharp electro-storm
in my chest (seedbed) a dead man
has taken, from his burial plot something is passed
across a clutching reaches out of the grave
a vestige of life (the memory of a rhythm), nothing
quantifiable, this sudden tilt into speed, my own
insinuating daemon go-between
of a different life, unhinged, chambers twitching
while weeping at this grave
i (heart-maggot) become the slowly
gnawed, from within
host of a dead man

jetzt kommen sie

jetzt kommen sie
jetzt kommen die hände wieder
im fensterausschnitt ein himmel
zwei, eine naht

jetzt kommen sie
jetzt kommen die arme wieder
mich umdrehen, rühren
dass ich mich nicht aufliege

jetzt kommen sie
jetzt kommen die schmerzen wieder
blutrausch im kopf, etwas
leicht atmendes

ein sich kaum regendes
schwarzes band am ärmel
der schwester, eingetragen
auf kassenrechnung klappernde
knochen, wie viele male
zuckende glieder

jetzt kommen sie
jetzt kommen sie wieder
männer mit händen wie schaufeln
jetzt komme ich, ein leichtes bündel
jetzt komme ich lebendig
ins grab

here they come

here they come
here come the hands again
in part of the window a sky
two, a seam

here they come
here come the arms again
turning me over, moving me
so i won't get bedsores

here they come
here come the pains again
rush of blood to the head, something
lightly breathing

a barely moving
black band on the nurse's
arm, registered
and accounted for rattling
bones, how often
twitching limbs

here they come
here they come again
men with hands like shovels
here i come, a light bundle
here i come alive
to the grave

für die nacht geheuerte zellen

2001

cells hired for the night

2001

jemand gab mir feuer
das ich gar nicht wollte
was sollte ich damit
(mitten in der nacht)
und ich rannte herum
in den autos saßen menschen
ihr atem beschlug die scheiben
die autos standen am straßenrand
und ich rannte um es
wieder auszublasen das feuer
bis ich einen schwarzen lichtschalter fand
in einem hotel am bahnhof
eine lampe schwankte um ihren arm
ein vogel pfiff (nacht) und das feuer
knisterte hinten (oder war es nah)
im umspannwerk ich hatte es doch
gelöscht im takt zzzt zttt zzzt knisterte
mein limbisches hirn
eine entwicklerwanne das dumme ding
und der vogel schrie sein zzzt zttt zzzt in die nacht
wo das feuer manchmal sich
kleine vögel briet es
roch überall die anderen
sagten dass das der frühling sei
das feuer spielte blitz
und war ein baum
dabei wurde es lose (mein hirn) und
ein hotel mit schwarzem lichtschalter
als ich
darauf drückte machte es pscht und tscht und
dann immer heller zzzt zzzt zzzt
sprang vom hirn in den bauch

somebody gave me a light
i didn't even want it
what good was it to me
(in the middle of the night)
and i rushed about
people were sitting in cars
their breath steaming up the windows
the cars were on the roadside
and i rushed about
trying to blow out the fire
until i found a black light switch
in a hotel near the station
a lamp was swaying on its arm
a bird whistled (night) and the fire
crackled at the back (or was it nearby)
in the substation surely i had put it
out my limbic brain
crackled zzzt zttt zzzt in time
a developer tank the stupid thing
and the bird screamed its zzzt zttt zzzt into the night
where the fire sometimes
fried little birds there was
a smell everywhere the others
said that was spring
the fire played at lightning
and was a tree
in doing so it came loose (my brain) and
was a hotel with a black light switch which
when i
threw it went psht and tsht and
then grew ever brighter zzzt zzzt zzzt
leaping from my brain into my belly

der kleine vogel briet
jetzt roch ich auch
dass es (doch) der frühling war

leipzig, märz 2000

the little bird fried
now i too smelled
that it (actually) was spring

leipzig, march 2000

kontaktlinsen

es war so: hell
die augen tränten ich stolperte
die bäuche überall readers' digest
im wartezimmer schrillendes: *optometrist* und
augapfelhaut gelb geädert die tapete die wand
tappte, ich, durchs dunkel zwischen bad und bett
brannte, ich, ja doch, „noch ungeküsst"
sie vergaßen mir zu erklären dass die dinger
verrutschen zwischen glaskörper und lid
tastend, tränend
mit fingern, weit aufriss, ich vorm spiegel
die linse dieses kleine grüne boot
mit all ihren bildern schon durch mein gehirn gleiten
sah –

pulte sie raus
setzte sie auf die fingerkuppe
und saugte die bilder von ihr

contact lenses

it was so: bright
my eyes watered i stumbled
the bellies everywhere reader's digest
in the waiting room shrillness: *optometrist* and
eyeball-skin yellow-veined the wallpaper the wall
padded, i, through the dark between bathroom and bed
burning, me, yes really, "still unkissed"
they forgot to tell me the things can
slide between vitreous and lid
probing, runny eye
at the mirror i, with fingers, opened wide
saw the lens this little green boat
with all its images already gliding
through my brain –

plucked it out
laid it atop my finger
and sucked in its pictures

glasbau, die schenkel

glasbaustein, etwas ansehen
gehen, im bad, rubbeln, abziehen
etwas lebendiges ansehen gehen
in anderen sprachen, im bad:
wachs an den beinen, bienenbänder
wie wesen? ein ratsch –
brennendes bein. die einzelnen
haare, krumme fühler
am band (was für musik
wäre das mit den
kleinen wurzeln und knoten
in alle richtungen
gedreht?)

doch jetzt, abgezogen
im siphon, in der schwemme
wesen, stumm. mücken
des verschlungenen
(nichts): knoten, wie
werden + sein. glasbau,
die schenkel, endlich
gespreizt. *werden.* nicht
nackt, nicht gedrungen.
jemanden mögen. mücke
und spinne am blühenden
glas, das eine nackte
das eine behaarte
bein. jäger und
beute. ich mag
dich sehr.
etwas
sein

glasswork, the thighs

glass component, going to see
something, in the bathroom, rubbing, peeling
going to see something living
in other languages, in the bathroom:
wax on legs, bee strips
what sort of be-ing? a rasp –
burning leg, the individual
hairs curly feelers
on the strip (what would you
call a music of little
roots and knots
twisted in all
directions?)

but now, picked off
in the siphon under the whirling torrent
beings, mute, mosquitoes
entwining to
(nothing): knots like
be-come + *be*. glasswork
the thighs, spread
at last. *becoming*. not
naked not stocky.
to like someone. mosquito
and spider on the blossoming
glass, one leg
peeled, one leg
hairy. hunter and
quarry. i like
you very much.
being
something

frühsprachen

die wiesen wären rot, die zungen grün
grün das blut, die bäume rot
gesichter vor freude grün
rot bei übelkeit, rot
der schimmel wie die wiesen
geriffelte schlünde grün
kupferspanrot die ampeln
wenn wir führen, rot
die wiesen, der schleim.
laufschriftbänder grün
wie früher die wiesen
die rot wären
wie früher
die zungen und gaumen
wären deine grünen augen
rot, ich rutschte hindurch
fingernägel wüchsen grün
wie blut, grün
die farbe des zorns, grün
bedeutete „herz", unser schleim
wäre rot, rot
wie hinter den ohren
glühwürmchen leuchteten grün
adern unter der haut
die grüne lippen berührten
brennnesseln wären rot
wie die bereitschaftslichter
der geräte, die grün wären, da die
wiesen rot wären, als wären sie
zungen gewesen, und der himmel
wäre noch immer blau
wir gingen aufrecht
du wärest hier

early languages

meadows would be red, tongues green
green the blood, the trees red
faces turn green with pleasure
red with nausea, fungus
as red as the meadows
ridged throats would be green
verdigris-red the traffic light
as we pulled away, red
the meadows, the phlegm
LED-tickers green
like the meadows once were
which would be red
just like tongues and palates
once were
your green eyes would be
red, i would get through it
fingernails would grow green
as blood, green
as the colour of anger, green
would stand for "heart", our phlegm
be red, red
like behind the ears
glow-worms would glow green
veins beneath the skin
be brushed by green lips
nettles would be red
like the stand-by lights in machines
which would be green, since the
meadows would be red, as if they'd
been tongues, and the sky
would still be blue
we would walk tall
you would be here

bläuliche sphinx (wolke

lied im bauch

schmerz; das sind die geschabten wände
im bauch
                              – leer geräumt, stillgestellt
in allen muskelfasern, in allen fasern
fehlt das kind –
                              im bauch. es gelten die gesetze
der reproduktion, sie machen geräusch, die
küretten, sie saugen sich fest
im keim, im dezember
                              – im bauch. krankentische
klappen herunter, weiß und geschabt, die
gesetze der hygiene gierig
sitzt der stöpsel im rücken der hand
                                                            – rotes
plastik und trinkt. was aber heißt
„wolke")
                              würzelchen, du.
auf dem gang wird gesungen
geschrubbt.
                    äste schrubben das fenster
die nacht. tritt herbei, zur wanne
zum heißen wasser
                              – im mensch.
der weint; in allen fasern mißt
seine weite (im auge, im herzen)
allein in der nacht
                              vermisst
die kleinen buchten, das kind.

bluish sphinx (cloud

song in the belly

pain; that's the scraped walls
in the belly
          – evacuated, rendered still
every fibre of every muscle
missing the child –
          in the belly. the rules of
reproduction prevail, they make a noise, the
curettes, they suck hard
on the embryo, in december
          – in the belly. bedside
tables flap down, white and scraped, the
rules of hygiene voracious
the plug sticks in the back of the hand
                    – red
plastic and drinks. but what is meant by
"cloud")
          tiny root, you.
they're singing in the corridor
scrubbing.
       branches scrub the window
the night. steps closer, to the tub
to the water, warm
          – in the human.
who weeps; every fibre gauging
her expanse (by eye, by heart)
alone in the night
          missing
the little bays, the child.

die eingebogenen
finger zur kehle wie
zum singen gereckt
da, an der wand
(eine wolke erst) bläuliche sphinx
fragen –
in allen fasern (allen
sprachen – sie klappen
herunter, sie klappen
herauf)
mit dem spiegel
der abgeschabten wand (die äste
am fenster) ungestillt.
fasern. auf stille gestellt.
doch hungrig, doch ragt
aus der hand der stöpsel
rot, ein leergeräumter mund
– unstillbar, im mensch.

the fingers
turned to the throat as if
stretching out to sing
there, on the wall
(a cloud at first) a bluish sphinx
questions –
in every fibre (in every
language – flapping
down, flapping
up)
with the mirror
of the scraped wall (the branches
at the window) unstilled.
fibres. rendered still.
yet hungry, yet the valve
protruding from the hand
red, an evacuated mouth
– unstillable, in the human.

op

(narkose)

morphiumbienen
ihre gelbschwarzen streifen
ein glibbriger klacks
in die vene gespritzt –
schon hebt sich ein haariges bein
senkt sucht (so sehr behaart)
(doch ohne flaum) ein zweites
(als wär es bestäubt)
das den steiß umschließt
den ausschießenden kopf
morphiumbienen
narkoseschwämmchen
tunken uns ein.

sie spritzen dich mir
zwischen den beinen
aus, kind, blümchen
„nackter strand“, je nachdem
es spult sich ab
in uns, wo „du“, strang
faser riss, als „lila licht“
vielleicht „dereinst“
auf einem hügel sitzt
„in diesen regionen“
pronomenlos
ein paar, unten, am strand
das dich wiederzeugt
während du
honigkugeln rollst
oder elektrizität oder gedanken
in der biene, in der spinne
im lichtlosen see.

op

(anaesthesia)

morphine bees
their yellow-blackish stripes
a slimy glob
squirted into the artery –
already a hairy leg lifts
sinks seeks (so very hairy)
(yet unfluffed) a second
(as if pollen-powdered)
encircling the coccyx
the sprouting head
morphine bees
petite narcotic spongettes
dunking us under.

they're syringing you
out between my legs
child, baby blossom
"bare beach", whatever
it's unwinding
inside us, where "you", torn
cord fibre, as "lilac light"
perhaps, "one day"
will sit on a hill
"in these parts"
pronounless
a couple, below, on the beach
conceiving you again
while you
roll balls of honey
or electricity or thoughts
in the bee, in the spider
in the lightless lake.

angehn

(missed abortion, aushub 80 gr)

abtritt auftritt anlauf
ständig aufge
sogen abluft
anlauf anlaut durch schwimm
bälle ein
aus
atem durch an den arm
getackerten plastik
schlauch erscheinung
gezittert die
liegt auf der hand
mit verkrampften fingern
vorm gesicht, halb verdeckten
pupillen umwachsen von
dunkelgrün wie seen singen
für die nacht geheuerte
zellen dir nach.
aber kein gott tritt auf
nur dieser elektrische
schlag an der nach unten
geöffneten schenkeltür, vertrocknende
noppen, flackern, flackern
im absaugwind
zwei ärmchen
an einer schüssel
voll schlaf.

take

(missed abortion, extract 80 g)

unset outset onset
steadily suc
                    ked extract
inrun onset through float
balls in
                          out
breath through the arm-
tacked plastic
tube manifestation
trembling in
the hand with
cramped fingers
in front of the face, half hidden
pupils ringed with dark
green growth like lakes sing
after you cells
hired for the night.
but no god appears
only this electric
shock to the downward-opened
thigh door, nubs
drying up, flicker, flicker
in the suction wind
two little arms
on a basin
                    full of sleep.

(ultraschallkontrolle,
kurz danach)

glaskammern sind
wir. stehen im
bad. funkeln
und sind. licht
bricht, die tür
schwingt. splittert
und steht. glas tut
was es kann. im
screen schwimmt
eine erinnerung. nur
blind. ein rauher sack
die luft. lagen von haut
auf dem gesicht. etwas
zittert und fragt.

(ultrasound scan,
shortly after)

glass chambers we
are. standing in the
bathroom. glistening
and are. light
refracts, the door
swings. splinters
and stands. glass does
what it can. on the
screen a memory
swims. only
blind. a coarse sack
the air. layers of skin
on the face. something
trembles and asks.

neu und alt gewusst

(am tag darauf)

wir haben doch den herzenssumm
im garten stehen, kirschen essen
kindlich und froh

wir haben doch den herzenssumm
amseln im gras, hände
streicheln   spielendes licht

die summe am ende wartet still
streichelt uns – und hat ihn
doch, den herzenssumm, in uns
                    und kaut die kirsche, still.

new and old known

(the following day)

but we have the heart's-hum
standing in the garden, eating cherries
childlike and cheery

but we have the heart's-hum
blackbirds in the grass, hands'
caress   play of light

the sum at the end waits, still
caresses us – and has it
really, the heart's-hum, in us
                    and chews the cherry, still.

(in der siebten nacht)

im traum gehen die hügel
von mir weg. sie sind
meine brüste. im traum
verliere ich was mir wert
kommt mir abhanden
die kerze der rosa strumpf
schlüssel und schuh. ich werde
pilzsucherin. ich gehe
ins feld, mit einem korb. vor mir
buddelt ein schwarzer hund.
heimlich über den rand eines hügels
gebeugt, sehe ich ihn, er gräbt
trüffel aus, das gelände ist dunkel
und roh. in weiten maschen hängt
mein roter pullover mir über den
bauch. eine warme hand legt sich
auf mein ohr. mein körper kommt
zu mir zurück. reißverschlüsse
schnappen an mir auf und zu.

(in the seventh night)

the hills in my dream are moving
away from me. they are
my breasts. in my dream
i lose the thing i value
i am unable to find
the candle the pink stocking
key and shoe. i become
a mushroom hunter. i take to
the fields with a basket. scraping
the ground ahead of me is a black dog.
leaning stealthily over the edge
of a hill i see it is digging
for truffles, the terrain is dark
and raw. my pullover loose-knit
and red hangs over
my belly. a warm hand covers
my ear. my body comes
back to me. zips on me keep
coming undone and doing up.

(in der achten nacht, traum)

sah sie ein
tampon einschieben
eine kleine weiße figur
eng gepackt wie zum fallschirmsprung – ein kinderfoto
erschien – die kleine als fliegenpilz – jemand drehte
den knopf – zitternder zeiger über leuchtendes
senderband – gehirntakt einer mücke beim
flug übern libellenteich.

das glatte. das gekerbte.
das glänzende, innen, in ihr.
propfverschluss. blutung nach *missed*
abortion. überm band phosphoresziert
im ultratraschall der zeiger
weiß: *follow me*
follow me. weiß wie ein zahn
liegst du in meinem bauch

und schläfst.

(in the eighth night, dream)

saw her
inserting a tampon
a small white figure
tightly packed as if for parachute jump – a photo of a child
appeared – little one as a fly amanita – someone turned
the knob – trembling needle over luminous
frequency scale – rhythms of a gnat's brain in
flight across a dragonfly pond.

the smooth. the notched.
the gleaming, inside, of her.
barrier plug. bleeding following *missed*
abortion. above the scale the pointer
in the ultrasound scan phosphoresces
white: *follow me*
follow me. white as a tooth
you lie in my belly

and sleep.

(am morgen)

… und weiches.
mit der schwarzen beere
im maul. wolltest
die welt nicht sehen
ihren leid
ihren schmerzens.
doch zärtlich sein
(brennende bäume, kind
die käfer
sind liebes, darin)

dir, mit der schwarzen beere
im maul.

(in the morning)

… and softness.
with the black berry
in your mouth. you did
not want to see the world
it's anguish
it's paining.
to be tender though
(burning trees, child
the beetles
so dear, in them)

to you, with the black berry
in your mouth.

ich frage dich, wer wir sind

(beim verlassen des krankenhauses)

kind:
knallorange das plastik
rettungsfahrzeug
zerhacktes holz, der fernsehturm
blinkte tag und nacht. frühstück im
bett. rot leuchteten die backsteine
akanthusblätter, aus stein.
eine embryowolke zog vorbei
(deutlich der kopf, der schwanz
dein herz). silbrig
frieren/schmelzen
schneegraupeln
im kies.

es ist braun grau grün und
weiß / lebenswasser ist es
gefroren
geschmolzen
                              so
fort

                              schnee
und er leuchtet
wie grind.

i ask you who we are

(on leaving the hospital)

child:
bright orange that plastic
emergency vehicle
chopped wood, the tv-tower
blinked day and night. breakfast in
bed. the bricks glowing red
acanthus leaves, in stone.
an embryo cloud floated past
(the head, the tail visible
your heart). silvery
soft hail
freezes / melts
in the gravel.

it is brown grey green and
white / water of life it is
frozen
melted
            there
and then

                        snow
and it gleams
like crust.

du

(drei monate später)

siehst du die wolke hoch oben, über der amsel, die saugende
sonne, daran? hörst die baumbüschel, die mistelzweige
siehst die nester im leeren geäst? ringsherum geht die zeit. hier
und da schneit es uns. auf die erde, als seelchen, im rock
des körpers, und froh. zwischen den blättern, siehst du
hüpft es im schnee, blinkt dich an. ein cyberjuwel, auf
dem gefieder der amsel. kristall, leichter als schnee.
die sonne schleckt daran. es summt. es sirrt. es ist
fiberglas, wie unter der erde, rot, wie in einer wand
mutter, in dir. wie du da sitzt und denkst: du.
dich drehst, wegdrehst, suchst, nach dem ast. er pocht
dir in der hüfte, unter der jeans. lied, das da sirrt. ich
bin so leicht, als kleines, weggegangen, von dir.

du hast es gekauft. zwei goldfische schwimmen darin. grün
wedeln die arme der algen hinterher. immer in dieselbe
richtung schwimmen die fische im glas, im kreis. ihre
schwarzen augen sind wie der mond. auch er hat
eine seite, die ist unsichtbar. das glas steht in deinem
bauch. du siehst mit der ader zwischen hüfte und
scham. ich schneie als winter ins zimmer hinein.
du lächelst. der mond, unsagbar, im zimmer drin.
kleine orange sterne schwimmen die fische um uns.

you

(three months later)

can you see that cloud high up, above the blackbird, the sun
sucking, on it? can you hear the tree tufts, the mistletoe twigs
see the nests in the empty branches? time goes round and round. here
and there it snows us. on the earth, as tiny souls, dressed
in our bodies, and glad. between the leaves, can you see
something frisking in the snow, blinking at you. a cyberjewel, on
the plumage of the blackbird. crystal, lighter than snow.
the sun licks it. it hums. it buzzes. it is
fibreglass, like under the earth, red, like in a wall,
mother, inside you. the way you sit there thinking : you.
turning, turning away, searching, for the branch. it throbs
at your hip, under your jeans. song, buzzing there. i
am so light, a little one, gone away, from you.

you have bought this. in it two goldfish swimming. green
weed waves its arms behind them. the fish in the bowl
always swim in the same direction, in circles. their
black eyes like the moon. it too has
a side that's invisible. the bowl is in your
belly. you see with the artery between hip and
vulva. i snow into your room as winter.
you smile. the moon, beyond words, in the room.
little orange stars the fish swim around us.

hiddensee, südstrand, die kämpfenden vögel

ziehst
im grünen rock, mit den bauchrollen (du)
das gelötete haar zum nest gesteckt
zellschlaf, ziehst
langer traum, ein
kleines mädchen, leptosom
mit gereckter kehle
an einer leine weinend
(rollend
rollen probend ...) hinter dir her
                                        – über den strand
                                        die schrift, lotophag, auch
                                        die und die nackten beine

hiddensee, south beach, the fighting birds

traipsing
in your green skirt with those tummy rolls (you)
your soldered hair pinned in a nest
cells dormant, pulling,
long dream, a
little girl, leptosome,
throat craning
weeping on a lead
(rolling
trying out roles …) behind you
                    – along the beach
                    the script, lotophagous, these
                    too and their bare legs

monitoring

im vergleich zu uns alt
gesprungener lack bohlen
weich verschmiert im vergleich dazu
wir, kernchen, hüllenlos.
dünne haut überm lack
des denkens und ichs –
verwohntes parkett – ich kratze
mit bloßer hand, bohle um bohle
rutsch ich auf knien voran
lösungsmittel im vergleich zu mir
teuer schnüffel ich
unterm schädel begriffe
ab, atme
leicht bin lebe
jetzt hier, um glücklich
zu sein   boote ich

abends das notebook hoch. schwärme
unbekannter vögel
polyvalente apparaturen
gleichmäßig geometrisch präsent
überm balkon saugen aus
der fuge im kopf
gedanken, lösen sich auf
an, wachsen, stürzen, herab?
handeln das einsatzgebiet: horch
nachts die bohlen, geschliffen, nackt
chatten mit dem metall über
mir, in mir, chips, im vergleich
zu uns konkret, mein
gehirn abstrakt im vergleich
von mir zu mir selbst. stelle

monitoring

old in comparison to us
cracked varnish floorboards
softly blurred in comparison
us, seeds, unwrapped.
thin skin over the varnish
of thinking and ego –
worn-down parquet – i scratch
with my bare hand, plank by plank
sliding forward on my knees
solvents in comparison to me
expensive i sniff
up concepts under my
skull, breathing
freely, am, live
here now in order to be
happy   i boot

up the notebook in the evening. flocks
of unfamiliar birds
polyvalent apparatuses
uniform geometric present
above the balcony suck thoughts
out through the seam
in my head, dissolve
solvate, grow, swoop, downward?
negotiate their field of operation: listen
the boards at night, sanded, bare
chatting with the metal above
me, in me, chips, in comparison
to us real, my
brain abstract by comparison
with me to myself. as a chip

es mir chip nur vor etwa dass
ich denke dachte ja bloß   um glücklich

zu sein, ein dicker käfer
die blauen flügel angelegt kriecht
durch mich hindurch die schalen
der begriffe hängen lose herab
der käfer klickt mit seinem
fühler das bombenfeld an. mit links,
fühler, die bomben. er sprüht
nicht ich. cyborgs gleiten
durchs bild, *human target*
handle with care

imagine it as this notion that
i think, thought merely   to be

happy, a fat beetle
its blue wings folded crawls
through me the shells
of concepts hanging loosely
as the beetle with its feeler clicks
on the bombing zone. a cinch
feeler, the bombs. it's it spraying
not me. cyborgs drift
through the picture, *human target*
handle with care

stoffen

wie bäume schmecken
und dass wir vögeln so nahe sind
(die mögen das auch) (kirschen, beeren)
dass bäume so unterschiedlich schmecken
sich für klein oder groß entschieden haben
– und was an süßer feuchtigkeit
und zahl der kerne zwischen kirschen
und birne
liegt
und dann die ragenden (klüftenden
                                        als wärs in einem wettbewerb, berge)
und birnbäumchen dazu (so klein) (auch die feldhacker)
und warum die johannisbeeren so
sauer die kirschen so süß (die vögel
fressens ja doch) und sie wachsen
in bündeln (beere und kirsche)
(die birne nicht) aber doch unterschiedlich
gereust (mit kopftüchern stehen sie da)
mehr wasser oder mehr dichte
so wachsen sie (für die vögel? für uns?)
denn wer säh die festigkeit der birne
dem baum an, so viel kleiner als die kirsche (die
aber mit ihren hängenden blättern)
wie er festes schiebt und
gehäuse im gehäuse baut, für den wurm, der
die birne fördert, wie den apfel
aber die kirsche nicht – ist sie also eher
luft? (wobei der verdacht dass wir
aus der sicht der bäume nur, wie vögel
samenverbreiter sind) – und die roten
eine eigene gruppe, wie bei ihnen die ästchen
und gezackten blätter auch der johannisbeere

to substances

the way trees taste
and we are so close to birds
(which they like too) (cherries, berries)
the way trees have such different tastes
have opted for small or tall
– and how sweet moistness
and number of seeds
varies between cherries
and pears
and then the towering (splitting apart
                    as if competing, mountains)
and their pear trees (so little) (and hackers in fields)
and why the redcurrants
are so bitter cherries so sweet (the birds
eat them anyway) and why they grow
in clusters (berries and cherries)
(but not pears) but are differently
netted (and here they are, in headscarves)
with more water or greater density
that's how they grow (for the birds? for us?)
for who could tell a pear's firmness
by the tree, so much smaller than the cherry (which
however with its hanging leaves)
the way it strives for firmness, fitting
its core with firmer chambers, for the worm
that nurtures the pear, as it does the apple
but not the cherry – so is it more like
air? (raising suspicions that we
if only from the trees' point of view, are
birdlike dispersers of seed) – and the reds
a discrete group, and the way their shoots
and serrated leaves, of currants too

aus säure wachsen, in süße schieben
grünes dessous über lackierter haut
ja, die häute, bei allen (die der kirsche
am zartesten, daher nicht für den wurm, sondern
für bakterien und dass also wir wie vögel
und bakterien einfach samenverbreiter sind)
und die häute – bei allen – die (so
schnell der sommer) der sonne entgegen
platzen –
          ganz kleine bäumchen
          werden, wieder, aus licht

growing out of bitterness, push for sweetness
green lingerie on lacquered skin
yes, the skins, of them all (the cherry's
the most delicate, therefore not for the worm but
for bacteria and so that we like birds
and bacteria are simply spreaders of seed)
and the skins – of all – which (as soon
as summer) explode into
the sun –
          very small trees
          growing, again, out of light

kugelblitz

2005

ball-lightning

2005

hiddensee, südstrand,
die winkende bucht
(hiddensee 2)

geht einer hier lang, licht?
hagebutten, ein haus, ein haupt
flockige pflanze, nach oben geweht

tang – lockig über den sand. violetter
geist, oder geist von was:
lächeln, wie licht, das auf einer

spitze steht, zerfressen, kichernd –
kindergesicht? mit höhligem wie
eine höhle schatten für schwalben

oder mückenstich, auch beulen
hautnah, sandig, eben: als licht.
etwas das geht taumelt dreht

gernhaben

eben und eben eben der strand
aus arbeit die reibt, sandig, lüstern
glänzend das meer, und flach

wir, dabei, in die luft gebaut. ein
violetter schatten, dort, oben
dies löchrige tuch ich spreche

dich

durch es. wenn ich sage "du". wenn
ich sage "ich wollte …" "ich …" ein
kindergesicht. oh gespenst! löchriger

hiddensee, south beach,
the beckoning bay
(hiddensee 2)

a walker along here, light?
rose hips, a house, a head
fluffy plant, seaweed upturned

by wind – curled across sand. violet
ghost, or ghost of what:
a smile, like light pitched

on a point, gnawed, a-giggle –
a child's face? with hollowy, like
a hollow shadow for martins

or mosquito bites, lumps too
skin-close, sandy, even: as light.
a thing that walks falters reels

cherishing

even so, and so even the beach
in its work of friction, sandy, wantonly
shining sea, and flat

us too, built in air. a
violet shadow, there, aloft
this porous fabric i speak

you

through it. if i say "you". if
i say "i'd like …" "i …" a
child's face. oh ghost! porous

busch: so sprech ich dich. wenn.
ich sage: du, eben, lüstern
und flach das meer. komm

sagst du
komm her.

shrub: i'll speak to you so. if.
i say: you, even, wanton
and flat the sea. come on

you say,
come here

entenbrust, rötlich,
die straße entlang

wie die straßenbahn sich kreischend
in die kleinste kurve schlang ihr
folgte nach die schaffnerin durchs
mikro kauderwelsch legte lachend
aus wie sie würde höllisch
hüftend – als der
rüde an der ecke die wollhaarige
hündin zum spiel auffordernd
täppisch ja flötend sie immer wieder
anrempelte mit den hüften
zart zur seite ihr lief auf
allen pfoten quer – sie aber
gähnte die zunge so
blau

kinder spielten das letzte
verstecken des tages

wie sauste die bahn nun
ganz gerade die straße hinab
wie schlug die spiegelung
ihrer fenster im asphalt
mit den flügeln

breast of duck, ruddy,
all down the street

the screeching tram the way it
took the tightest of curves
the conductress following her
through the mike gibberish
expounding laughing how she
hellishly hip – as the
      dog on the corner
urged the frizzy bitch to play
gauchely even sweetly bumped
his hips against her over and again
minced along beside her all
paws square – and she just
      yawned her tongue so
                  blue

kids played their last
hide-and-seek of the day

the way the tram whizzed now
dead straight down the street
the way the reflection
of its windows in the tarmac
          beat its wings

nähe von maschinen

er brachte den velo-sattel hoch dunkles seepferdchen an der wand
schon mal tiere gesehen die sich anschreien nur um zusammenzusein
die tiefkühltruhe summte schnelleres abtauen mit föhn

wie er später eingekesselt als käfer und sie auf dem fahrrad
wo röhren in einen übergehen sah etwas wie *bolliger mops*
mit blumentopfrücken erde darin augen drehten auf fühlern

schneckengleich. er sprang in die küche rollte sich ein –
vor den maschinen. der spüler im vollprogramm. es machte ihr angst
so überinstrumentiert zu sein – andererseits all die gesparte zeit

sie dachte wie solch ein tier wohl schläft mit dem blumentopfrücken
und sah mit braunem zucker bestreut all das verträumte trara
(angeblich des traums) aber sofort war er wach (die ohren) sofort

fiel er wieder um wie ein kind – wie es weint – alle
gefühle also seien erlernt auch unter ihrer straff
gespannten bluse sitze fell leberfarbene haut poche

dunkles tier an der wand, ein wässriges herz?

proximity of machines

he brought up the bike-saddle a dark sea-horse on the wall
ever seen animals screaming at each other just to be together
the deep freezer hummed defrosting faster with a dryer

later the way he was trapped as a beetle and she on the bike
where tubes become one with the body saw a kind of *clumpy pug*
with a flowerpot back soil in it eyes twisting on feelers

snail-like. he dashed into the kitchen curled up in a ball –
in front of the machines. washing machine on full cycle. so much
over-instrumentation frightened her – but then again the time saved

she wondered how an animal like that slept with its flowerpot back
and saw sprinkled with brown sugar all his dreamy to-do
(supposedly the dream's) but he woke up at once (those ears) at once

falling over again like a child – cried like one – so
all feelings were learnt even under her tightly stretched
blouse there was fur liver-coloured skin dark

animal throbbing on the wall, a watery heart?

kugelblitz, hammondorgel

aber sie sei
aber sie sei gestorben
aber sie sei wiedererweckt
also erstanden – *in der küche*
beim teigrühren getroffen beim
puddingkochen gelb in diesen topf
gebullert, gnade, galle auch feuerqualle –
aber sei sie hingeschlagen
leicht nur berührt an der stelle
wo eine hirnader nervenhaut über
… den hof gesaust mit zwei leeren plastiksäcken
herzsäcken geradeaus schwebend *in der luft*
mit den pochenden säcken sich zugleich
an der küchendecke ganz oben in eine ecke
gekauert das gelbe brodeln im topf das laue
wehen des plastiks im hof *erkannt*
ihn da unter sich am einschlagsort kniend
eingeschlagen in trauer, florett, ein fechten wollen
die säcke überm hof flatternd als riefen sie sie
weil
    und weil
            dieses sein leibesheulen am herd ein flehender
amselschnabel so gelb und zart sie gespürt berührt sei sie
wieder eingefahren also wiedererstanden in der küche
auf dem boden die augen bang über quer den hof
sauste ein sperling so aber sei sie
so aber sei sie
geblieben eine narbe am knie
unscheinbar – 20 sekunden
weiblicher odysseus von blitzreise
eine haarsträhne ringelt sich
in ihren ausschnitt das

ball-lightning, hammond organ

but surely she
but surely she died
but surely she was roused
and so has risen – struck
in the kitchen while stirring the pastry
while cooking pudding yellow it *roared*
into the pot, mercy, gall and fire jelly –
but apparently fell over just lightly touched
where brain artery and nerve tissue over
… the yard, hurtling with two empty plastic bags
heart sacs floating straight *through the air*
with those throbbing bags all at once
cowering in a corner up on the kitchen
ceiling recognized the yellow bubbling in the pan
the sickly wafting of plastic in the yard
him there below her kneeling at the strike-point
stricken, grieving, foiled, bent on a fight
the bags aflutter over the yard as if calling her
because
    and because
        she'd sensed his body-howling at the cooker a pleading
blackbird's beak so yellow and tender she was touched
and had returned that is risen again in the kitchen
on the floor her eyes fearful crossing above the yard
flashed a sparrow but thus it is true she
but thus it is true she
stayed, a scar on her knee
unremarkable – 20 seconds
of female ulysses on a lightening tour
a strand of hair curling
into her cleavage its

blond jetzt braun gefärbt
so sei sie übers meer *gezirpt*
sie meine *gezippt*

blond now tinted brown
    and so it was she *zizzed* across the sea
                    says she meant *zipped*

eins reicht in die erde hinunter zu eichen

wurzeln, ist da geknotet. der andere
hat beine aus luft, luftiger als luft, stelzen
darin. ein dritter denkt und sehnt sich
nach fischweibern. wo hört auf der bogen
des balls wie geht er entlang in der luft
ohne die erde zu verlassen als satz.
die blume im fenster nun wo es dunkel ist
stellt den geist einer blume neben sich.
männer die bier trinken sehen immer
gleich aus. ein tropfen fällt, in sich ein
ganzes haus, es ist rosa und hat fenster
im dach. davor spielt ein paar federball
ein hund steckt den kopf durch den zaun.
bäume können nicht weglaufen. ein vogel
sein gefalteter schnabel, das täschchen.
die säge füllen holzarbeiter mit benzin.
der hund japst im schlaf und zuckt
mit den beinen. seine träume sind
nüsse. wir sehen die schale. der hund
ist die schale des traums. wir greifen
ihn am losen fell. falls dies stimmt

wird auch das paar eine vermutung **sein**

one reaches into the earth to oak

roots, is knotted there. the other
has legs of air, airier than air, stilts
therein. a third is in thought and longs
for fishwives. where will the ball's
arc end how can it go along in the air
without leaving the earth with a leap.
the flower in the window where it's dark
places the ghost of a flower next to itself.
men drinking beer always look
the same. a drop falls, in itself a
whole house, it is pink and has sky-
lights. a couple play badminton at the front
a dog sticks its head through the fence.
trees cannot run away. a bird
with its crossed bill its little bag.
tree surgeons fill the saw with fuel.
the dog yaps in its sleep its legs
twitch. its dreams are nuts. we
can see the shell. the dog is
the shell of the dream. we clutch
at its loose fur. if this be true

the couple too is guesswork al**one**

kann ihn ja
nicht zwingen
nicht mal ... zu nichts

eine station mitten im wald. es
schneite. der marder sprang unter
sprühästen augen entlang. war
gar nicht da. wir waren wie schnee
hell weiß schnell. warfen mit bällen
auf nichts. wünsche wohl
wolken von uns. ein eichhörnchen
drehte die nuss im maul wie
eine wolke ihren graupel, über uns.
wer … wer wir … sah spuren. aus
weichen tüchern flackerte nördliches
licht nach einer schlange benannt
schien es zu fließen. legte jemand wort
für uns ein? das eichhörnchen drehte
die nuss eifrig wie wir das wort "nuss"
im gehirn. kiefernsamen sprang um
eine pfütze. wo die wolke gewesen
lagen am morgen baumstämme
sauber gesägt. im zimmer harz
wir tranken tee. elchpaté
stand auf dem tisch. im tee
schwamm eine kardamom drehte
sich, wolke, zu mir, du sagtest
du: die kommt jetzt, die
blüht jetzt, die
reiß ich frei

can't
force him
not even ... to nothing

stop-over in mid-forest. snow
fell. the marten sprang beneath
the sprays eyes and on. was
not even there. we were like snow
bright white quick. throwing balls
at nothing. wishes probably
clouds of ourselves. a squirrel
turned a nut in its mouth like
a cloud its hailstones, above us.
who … who we … saw tracks. out of
soft sheets flickered the northern
lights named for a serpent appearing
to flow. was somebody putting in
a word for us? the squirrel eagerly
turned the nut likewise we
the word "nut" in our brains. pine seed
sprang around a puddle. where the cloud
had been tree trunks lay in the morning
cleanly cut. resin in the room
we drank tea. moose pâté
was on the table. a cardamom
floated in the tea turning
a cloud, to me, you said
you: it's coming now, it's
blooming now, this
                                        i'll tear free

coventry

aber es war ja gar nichts zu sehen
                                        aber es waren ja
nur diese steine gras diese sonne
ein plombierter zahn es war ja
gar nichts zu sehen nur diese
bündel grüne blitze diese sonnige
sonne es war ja: nur das wetter nur ein
kaputter zahn zähne es war ja nichts
zu sehen an solch einem zahnlosen
plombierten es war ja ein angelnder platz
mit einer meute implantierter leute aus stein
es war ja ein traum er war ja nicht farbig
es war ja gar nichts zu sehen nur das gras
diese trauerbüsche gedankenamalgam
                                                            ins gemüt
heimgearbeitetes steinpublikum das gewissen
es war ja ein nagelnd angelndes bett es
war ja so englisches: sonnenwetter es war
ja gar nichts zu sehen

coventry

but there was really nothing to see
                    but there were
only these stones grass that sun
a filled tooth there was
nothing to see at all just these
sheaves of green lightning that sunny
sun there was: just the weather just a
bust tooth teeth there was nothing
to see in such a toothless filled in
thing was just an angling square with
a mob of implanted people in stone
a dream after all not in colour
nothing there to see just the grass
these weeping bushes thought-amalgam
                              home-wrought
into the soul stony spectators the conscience
was a nailing angeling bed it was
so engleashy: sunny weather there was
really nothing at all to see

nasse alpen

lieg knirschend
in den gummischalen eine
frau im hermelin nimmt
mir die kleinen organe ab
amygdala ein bisschen nieren
schaum. ich habe die spreng
träume (wieder) gehabt das
flixe sehen: wie eine
gruppe halbnackter sich gegen
eine tribüne lehnte schuppen ihre
zarten körper und die dunkelhaarige
mit ihren händen einen geist
aus der erde zum
sprechen brachte: er stieg
aus der in uns
geschürften stelle
rauchte dotterfarbene asche
die in den lungen raschelte
wie gift oder eine lösung manche
leuchteten davon eroberten
die rekorde der schanzen andere
stachen sich die münder an fichten
und tauchten zur kühlung in ton
ich aber froh ganz hinten
gewesen zu sein erkannte
halbwach dass alles fake
die sprengung inszeniert
einer an einem fernen knopf
hatte ausgelöst

dennoch musste ich bezahlen
es wird wohl später gewesen sein

wet alps

lie grating
in the rubber shells a
woman in ermine removing
my small organs
amygdala a little kidney
foam. i've had blast
dreams (again) fluid
vision: the way a group
of semi-nudes leant against
a stadium their delicate
bodies scaling and with her hands
the black-haired woman raised
a spirit of the earth
to speech: up it rose
from the place in us
that had been scraped
smoked yolk-coloured ash
that rustled in our lungs
like poison or a solution some
were aglow with it broke
records at the ski-jumps others
pricked their mouths on spruces
and bathed in clay to cool
but I glad to have been
at the back saw
half-awake that all was fake
the blast staged
someone at a distant button
had let off

but still I had to pay
it would probably have been later

die abgabe der kleinen organe
und ein nur leichtes verschieben
des blaus auf dem hang
dem ich begegnete
zu grün

zu nächst

the ceding of my small organs
and only a slight shifting
of the blue on the slope
which i encountered
too greenly

too begin with

hyazinthenkolik

du schliefst noch ich saß
dein atem ging der tag
schob wald ans feld
die wiese fing zu blitzen
an in schatten fraß ein
taubenpaar heiß die krallen
ihr ihm ein kleiner fleck am
hals. weich noch ihre rufe
wie kindheitsmorgen schön
(wenn alles schlief nur sonne
nicht und taube und das leise
dach) du gingst die brust geölt
gingst nackt die scheibe traf
ihn an der stirn gekühlt gewärmt
erstarrt. versuchen ist ein
spielen schuld und jedes bett
am boden hart im topf
die hyazinthe probt
ob ihren duft ganz
ohne dich ich trag

hyacinth colic

you were still asleep i sat
your breath was going day
was pushing forest fieldward
the meadow now began
to flash in shadows fed a
pair of pigeons her claws
hot him with a small fleck
on the neck. still soft their calls
as dear as childhood mornings
(when all was asleep but sun
and dove and the quiet
roof) you went your chest oiled
went nude the disc had struck
his forehead cooled warmed
hardened. trying is a
game guilt and every bed
on the floor is hard in its pot
the hyacinth is testing
out whether quite without you
i'll bear its scent

aufkommen

über den feldern der kleine fleck
wie er sich bog über die langen
sheddächer der lager wie
schnell er war dass das unsere
geschwindigkeit sei glaubte
das mädchen neben mir nicht
– angst flügel ein rumpf
zoomten auf uns zu
als ziehe jemand mit
schnellem seil uns
hinab wie die bäume
loderten im bruchteil
einer sekunde der räder
                                        touch down
sie sagte auf der erde sein heißt
seinen schatten berühren

coming down

above the fields the little speck
the way it curved across the long
sawtooth roofs of the depots
how fast it went the girl
beside me could not believe
that this was our own speed
– fear wings a fuselage
zooming towards us
as if someone with
rapid rope were pulling
us down the way the trees
blazed for a fraction
of a second of the wheels'
            touchdown
being on earth she said means
touching one's shadow

treppauf, treppab, zahm will ich sein

(er und sie)

die dreiecke bedecken ein system das sie rollen lässt
der teil den man sieht führt immer nach oben
der teil den man nicht sieht führt immer nach unten
sie beherrschte es perfekt: draufspringen, runter.
                                        alles war binär.
                                        rolltreppe.
schon das hatte lange genug gedauert – ich meine
es ihr beizubringen – bis sie sich die pfote quetschte
in brüssel. und wie teuer. manchmal kann
man schuld abschälen wie eine bananenschale.
                                        manchmal
                                        nicht. auch
das erscheint sowohl reichlich. als auch binär.
an dieser stelle band sich jemand einen schuh.
menschenzehen sind käsig und weich. jetzt nehmen
wir den lift. er bringt uns auf jeden gipfel
                                        auf skiern fährt
                                        man hinab.
die weiße flanke des berges ist nur außen zu sehen.
an dieser stelle fuhr jemand in meiner erinnerung
einen ganzen tag mit einem sessellift den immergleichen
berg hinauf. am abend sagte meine mutter: das war ein
                                        schöner tag
                                        du bist so braun.
jemand bindet sich den schuh über der kralle
so zu dass das dreieck zwischen den seitenschäften
und der zunge zu lachen scheint. rising and falling
sagst du. lach doch mal richtig, dann verschwindet
                                        dein verstand.
                                        gern lauf ich
nach. auf zwei beinen, binär. perfekt bedecke ich
das system das mich rollen lässt. der teil den man sieht

upstairs, downstairs, i want to be tame

(him and her)

the triangles cover a system that makes them roll
the bit you see always leads up
the bit you don't see always leads down
she was an expert: hopping on, hopping off.
                    everything was binary.
                    an escalator.
even that had taken its time – i mean
teaching it to her – till she went and crushed
her paw in brussels. that was dear. sometimes
you can peel off guilt like a banana-skin.
                    sometimes
                    not. that
too seems both plentiful. and binary.
at this point someone tied their shoelace.
human toes are cheesy and soft. we'll use
the lift now. it can take us to any peak
                    you can get
                    down on skis.
the white mountainside can only be seen outside.
at this point someone in my memory went
up the same mountain in a chairlift all day
long. in the evening my mother said: that
                    was a nice day
                    you are so brown.
now someone ties a shoe over their claw
so tight the triangle between the side shafts
and tongue seems to laugh. rising and falling
you say. come on, a proper laugh then you'll lose
                    your mind.
                    i follow with
pleasure. on two legs, binary. expert in covering
the system that makes me roll. the bit

führt immer nach unten. der teil den man nicht sieht
führt niemals nach oben. ich lache. kleine
                                                blaue äffin, kleiner
                                                affe, in blaue hosen
gesteckt. tierarztkosten immens

you see always leads downward. the bit you don't
see never leads up. i laugh. little
                    blue monkey her
                    little monkey him
in blue trews. vet's bills immense

rüde erben, brütendes meer

wie ein meer in ausbrütung tut wasser uns nichts
nur als zugefügtes vielleicht, dort über der tür.
dort über der tür den schwan abwischen, komm
schnell. er hängt sonst den hals in den erdplattenspalt
und frisst eine magnetische tablette. dann rasen wieder
finger aufeinander zu die sich nicht greifen wollen und es
ist als schnellte in einer badewanne ein brett 10
meter nach oben. nun verstehst du warum von der
tür die rede war. der schwan ist kein schwan sondern
ein schiff das seitlich schäumend fliegt. auf dem dach
liegt ein ruder. die türen des hauses schwimmen wie
tritte nun unter dem gras. ich fragte nach dir und sah
wie ermüdet du allein vom schwanmenü an der tür
bereits warst. der schwan war kein schwan sondern
ein ständig nach unten türmendes bild. erpelpenisse
zeigen widerhaken das ist bei vögeln nicht üblich.
manche ente ertrank bei der folgenden vergewaltigung.
in etwa: wasser ist sanft. in notfischlagern auch.
schau nur wie du geworden bist und an kokosmatten
geklammert. komm schnell, das glas abwischen über
der tür. jemand hat eier dort abgelegt. wir sind noch
in der ausbildung, sehr wahr. doch das gift eines
einzelnen davon steuerlos bestürmten nagels ist klein

rude heirs, brooding sea

like a sea hatching something up water won't harm us
only as inflicted perhaps, above that door.
the swan above that door come on wipe it off
quick. elsewise it will dip its neck in the tectonic
fault and gobble a magnetic tablet. then fingers
will rush towards each other again and fail
to get a grip and it will be like a board in a bath
rocketing 10 metres into the air. now you know why
there was talk of a door. the swan is no swan
but a ship in foaming lateral flight. lying on the roof
an oar. the doors of this house float like duckboards
now below the grass. i asked after you and saw
how tired even the swan-menu on the door had already
made you. the swan was no swan but an image
making off constantly downwards. the drakes'
penises display barbs suchlike is not usual in birds.
there were ducks drowned in the ensuing rape.
roughly: water is soft. in emergency fishing camps too.
just look what's become of you and clinging to coconut
mats. come on quick, wipe the glass down
above the door. someone has deposited eggs here. we're
still in training, true. but the poison of a single nail
subjected to the rudderless assault of that is slight

verfolgung, den berg hinauf hinab, in freier natur

der wille darf nicht eisern sein sondern biegsamer stab
wie eichhörnchen den rücken des gegners hinauf und ihn
dann zwischen den schultern nagt. eichhörnchen schimpfen laut
wenn sie die nuss nicht finden, die still vergrabene. aber was
radelst du dort in den büschen? oder sind das wirklich
verstecke, im blut versteckbare stoffe des wachsens
und eines heimlichen schlürfens in den traum hinein?
wo trikots leuchten wie küsse aus geld. allein die beine
strampeln den berg hinauf – hinab lässt sich fliegen
der helikopter zeichnete seine und deine geschwindigkeit
auf. die felder hellbraun, eine struppige natur, die spur
deines schweißes machte sie milder, vielleicht, oder
sollte der gegner darauf rutschen? nichts half
als zu warten auf einen tag der schwäche des anderen.
seinen schatten sahst du zuerst, als er dich überholte
so eng kroch er als sein eigenes bild an deinen speichen
entlang. wir lagen auf der couch, einer sagte
geschaut hättest du wie ein frisch geficktes
eichhörnchen – und ach, die augen, die knöpfe
sprangen dir über die straße davon

pursuit, up the mountain down, in the great outdoors

the will should not be iron but a supple pole
just as squirrels climb upon their rivals' backs then
gnaw between their shoulder blades. the squirrel scolds loudly
when it cannot find its nut, so peacefully interred. but
what are you cycling in the bushes for? or are they
really hidey-holes, substances concealable in blood
fostering growth and furtive shuffles into your dreams?
where jerseys gleam like moneyed kisses. legs alone
slog up the hill – the way down can be flown
the helicopter recording his speed and your
own. light brown fields, nature all unkempt, your
sweat tracks making it mellower perhaps or were
they meant for your opponent to skid on? nothing
for it but to wait for the other's weaker days.
you first saw his shadow when he overtook you
so closely did he creep as the image of himself past your
spokes. we were lying on the couch, someone said
you had had the look of a freshly fucked
squirrel – and oh, your eyes, those buttons
took a flying leap down the road

daddy longbein

und sie sagten
wie er immer immer
zahle sagten dass er
einmal komme lange hin
wie er niemals niemals

trinken würde tee. ich
drehte eine zog dann er
wie er niemals niemals?
nachts schwamm ein
mond das zimmer um

wie er immer immer
sagten sie ich roch an
seiner haut und schwoll
niemals niemals fällt
hier schnee. flaschen

brachen licht wie finger
wie er niemals niemals
drehte meine locken aus zog
daran wie er immer immer
sagten sie diese finger

beim abschied über
wangen wände sagte er
dass er niemals niemals
(dass er niemals niemals)
wie er immer immer sagten sie

daddy longbein

and they said
the way he always always
paid they said he'd
come some distant day
the way he never never

would drink tea. i rolled
one dragged then him
the way he'd never never?
at night a moon
swam round the room

the way he always always
so they said i smelled
his skin and swelled
never never snow
fell here. bottles

broke the light like fingers
the way he never never
twirled my curls and drew
them out the way he always always
so said they these fingers

taking leave across the cheeks
the walls he said
he never never
(that he never never)
the way he always always so said they

taucher, radebrech

(vom vierfachen sinn der schrift)

anzüge mit füßen hingen
am geländer, im trockner
hingen köpfe

je weiter ein boot entfernt ist
umso tiefer nach unten muss man
um es zu hören

mit dem andrang der schwärze
gegen die maske vorm gesicht

ertrinken, verstehen

diver, mangle

(of the fourfold sense of scripture)

suits with feet hung
over the railing, heads
hung in the dryer

the more remote the boat
the deeper down you need to go
to hear it

as the blackness presses in
on the mask before your face

drown, understand

fahren durchs holz, die geschachtelten halme

die stämme, zerkleinert, geloggt
(brandenburgholz) die weichen kiefern auf
langhölzer die sich biegen gelegt schlitten
im wald auf den sommer zu jenes miniaturhafte
blümchen zwischen nadeln zwischen letztem und
neuem jahr kleiner als ein fingernagel drei knospen sehr rot
wie vergossen und tänzelnd die freude – dieses donnern
über den waldboden das hochgeschreckte
reh der jagende terrier geräusch für sekunden
stille
als wäre gezappt das panorama, später jägerlied
terrier hechelnd im sand
die kleine blume wirklichkeit
(je nach größe) unberührt

(und wo leckt sich das reh?)

through the woods, the nested stalks

the trunks, chopped, logged
(brandenburg timber) the soft firs laid
on tall and pliable logs sledges
in the forest bound for summer that miniature
flower between needles between last and
new year smaller than a fingernail three buds very red
like joy spilling and skipping – this thundering
across the floor of the forest the startled
deer the terrier in full chase a second-long noise
stillness
as if the panorama had been switched, later
a hunting song a terrier panting in the sand
the tiny flower of reality
(depending on size) untouched

(and where licks the deer, leaks?)

berührte orte

2008

touched places

2008

dorf ohne straße

marmorn heruntergebrochen
vom berg schimmert der hof
unter der sonnenbirne, wasser
gleich. menschen hier jeden
tag zerbrochen wieder zusammen
gesetzt. alle arglosigkeit vertrieben
selbst aus hunden aus ziegen
den bäumen die nackt und hellgrau
unterm himmel stehen afrikas
sonne, dunstig, grünbrüstig
reich

einzelne bäume klettern
den berg hinauf, aus kuhhorn
ist der kamm gemacht der
strommast schief, neu, weiß
staken mandelblüten im gras
stochrig wie der hunger
im spatz

  DORF OHNE STRASSE
  neben bergen die riesiger
  schutt

sind

schutt der
langsam wandert
in summe kalter stein
der flüstert

  DORF OHNE STRASSE
  nachts schwimm
  ich längst

village with no street

quarried from the mountain
the marmoreal courtyard shimmers
like water beneath the grand-soleil
pear. people broken here
every day and put back
together. guilelessness driven
even out of dogs goats
the trees standing naked and light gray
under the sky africa's
sun, hazy, green-breasted
rich

single trees climbing
the mountainside, the comb
is cow-horn the pylon
lopsided, new, the blossoming
almonds stalk through the grass
tetchy like hunger
in a sparrow

    VILLAGE WITH NO STREET
    among mountains that are
    gigantic

debris

debris that
slowly wanders
all of it cold stone
that whispers

    VILLAGE WITH NO STREET
    by night i am already
    swimming

irrweg, irrregel
betelgeuze in
tausend sternen
über dir

Hoher Atlas, Tirzha

astray, runaway
betelgeuse among
a thousand stars
above you

High Atlas, Tirzha

arabisch die küste ihr weiches, verhalten

sie wandern als herde
wie nützlich ist evolution
und wasser gräbt stein wie
ein krieg selbst wenn er lange
vergangen ist. wir essen mit dem mund
wir haben zwei hände und doch
wachsen unsere herzen wie kristall oder
strom. danach unterscheiden wir
wer tötet wer getötet wird dünne
pfefferminzstangen und bonbons
explodieren im hirn. nur kamele kauen
kakteen, wir ziehen weiches vor und
bringen von den bergen blau gelb eine
blume die wir nicht aushalten
so klein ist sie. das schaf ruft
jeder organismus schmeckt eben
eigen. am langsamsten wachsen
die kristalle der computer
schwarzweiße welt
    die auch wir nun betreten
    köpfe auf bilder gesteckt
    tragen wir über mauern uns
    her

morgen blüht ginster
und gläsern umschließt die stadt
das meer

Assilah

arabic the coast its mellowness, subdued

they roam as a herd
how useful evolution is
and water gouges stone like
a war even when it's long
past. we eat with our mouths
we have two hands and yet
our hearts grow like crystals
or currents. which is how we decide
who kills who is killed thin
peppermint sticks and sweets
explode in the brain. only camels chew
cactuses, we prefer mellowness and
from the mountains bring blue yellow a
flower we cannot resist
it's so small. the sheep calls
every organism has its own
taste. the slowest to grow
are the crystals in computers
black and white world
    which we too have entered
    heads mounted on images
    parading ourselves across
    walls

tomorrow gorse will bloom
and the glassy sea embrace
the town

Assilah

wege im dunkeln entfliegen dem schlaf

hörte sie rufen auf den tag
genau im mandarinfarbenen
himmel berlins blind ich rufend
sie sah ich um eins in der
nacht auch andere an fenstern
stürze paare laut da am himmel
der allein von außen
über der stadt hing in ihrem
schmutzigen glockenschein
                                        die geister der gänse

                                        nimm, gern, als bild
das summen ihrer flügel im inneren
der säulen roms oder unter den
ästen eines traums
den wir in diesen parks auf bergen
die bunker waren denkmale
wurden die schwimmen auf drogen
kondomen und bier unter himmeln
die jeden stern schluckten
                    nimm
wohin wir stürzen
                    indem wir fahren
auffahren:
                                        im winter allein

                                        wege im dunkeln
entfliegen dem schlaf und später möchten
wir fragen das eis ob es noch sich erinnert
wie es als wasser war als stern als
stein als ich …
                                        als es fiel

paths in darkness fly from sleep

heard them calling one year later
to the day in the mandarin-coloured
sky over berlin me blind them
calling saw at one in the
morning others too at windows
ledges couples loud against
a sky which only from without
hung over the town in its
manky bell-jar glow
          these ghosts of geese

          take, if you like, this image
of their whirring wings inside
the columns at rome or under the
boughs of a dream
which we in these parks on mountains
that were bunkers became memorials
swimming in drugs
condoms and beer under skies
that swallowed every star
     take
to wherever we fall
     as we fare forth
start up:
          alone in winter

          paths in darkness
fly from sleep and later we want
to ask the ice if it remembers
what it was like as water as a star as
a stone as i …
          as it fell

und träumte von gänsen die rufen vor
einem stück angefahrenen augfarbenen
himmel über berlin mitte oktober
wir renkten die hälse, der himmel
ein tupf, die unterseite
eines schnabels

unfasslich heiser
                    uns
                    fauchend gestreckt

and dreamt of geese calling
near a patch of heckled eye-tinted
sky over berlin in mid-october
we craned our necks, the sky
was a blotch, the underside
of a beak

incomprehensibly raucous
          stretched towards us
          hissing

bayrisch-seeland
(ödelchen)

das war der golden zittrige staub: auf den wegen
den rainen die kleinen christusschädel gespalten
– auch da unten der süden die berge der schatten
hatten ein meer.
            wir wollen schnaps brennen gehen, birnen kehren
wieder im kirchgelb, türme tragen zwiebeln. von erde
zu träumen war stoff. großvater s. nahm die hände der frauen
die er fing
            ab in gips. über die wiesen den großporigen staub
sprang manche ihm davon. millischeckerl. katzenpratzerl.
was zukam lag händisch im speicher weiß träumende finger
kaum träumte
            er. mächtig beim kloster schimmerten durch den karfiol
die seelen des dorfs. eine sau warf ferkel in allen regenwurmfarben
und schnürlregen verband die oberen und unteren provinzen
bayrisch –
            seeland. was rutscht der friedhof am hang und die felder
verdreht ein einfacher laut wie w– w– wetterbleaml den hiasigen
hinnigen den vierteldenseinen mir kopf ziehen die wolken über
die geodelten wege
            den liebenden staub

bavarian lakeland
(mucked odelette)

here was the golden flickering dust: on the paths
the verges the little christ's-heads cracked
– and down there too the south the alps the shadow
had a sea.
          let's moonshine schnapps, pears are turning
church-wall yellow, towers sport onions. dreaming of dirt
was material. grandfather s. took the hands of the women
he caught
          in plaster of paris. some of them bolted across the meadows
through large-pore dust. pish-the-bed. pussytoes.
his part lay to hand in the attic, fingers dreaming in white
the second
          he dreamt. imperious through cloister cauliflower shimmered
the souls of the village. a sow littered in all the colours of the rain-worm
and endless drizzle united the upper and lower provinces
bavarian
          lakeland. how the hillside graveyard slips and the fields
turn at a single sound like cra-cra-craw's-toes our folk's
your folk's the gran-kids' my head too the clouds' pull
over the mucked paths
          this loving dust

revontulet

tausend kilometer weiter nördlich eben
rosa
schlangenlinien ziehen über den himmel
dunkelrot
graublau, himmel und lichter tanzen berg am
horizont
ziehen krähen in schwärmen entlang oder was
immer
das ist kähne schwanken und schreien und der himmel
wird
immer dunkler heller immer niedriger höher alles in
einem
wir sind 16 und wundern uns hier ist der
norden
boreas corona setz dir die flasche auf
lass
los hier ist norden hier sitzt man nicht
draußen
sondern im sand in den moosen und
wringt
die kissen aus waren sie nachts draußen wurden sie
vergessen
war draußen das aufsteigende das kletternde
meer
was reicht klettert im rücken wo fahren wir
hin
sag „himmel“ sag nähe wir waren 16 trafen
uns
in der küche das passte das passte kaum wir die
großen
und draußen saß keiner saß einer der erwartete uns
er

revontulet

a thousand kilometres further north these
pink
wavy lines snake across the sky deep
red
grey-blue, sky and lights dancing a hill on the
horizon
crows streaming past in flocks or what-
ever
that is boats wobble and yelling and the sky
getting
ever darker brighter ever lower higher all at
once
we are 16 and amazed so this is the
north
boreas corona put the bottle on your head
let
go this is north you don't just sit outside
here
you sit in the sand in the moss
wringing
out pillows if they were left out all night been
forgotten
was outside the rising the climbing
sea
what's enough climbs behind you where shall we
go
say "sky" say closeness we were 16 met
in
the kitchen it was fine was hardly right we the big
kids
and no one sitting outside one sat waiting for
us

war noch klein ein flacher frosch mit dem auge an der
seite
dem auge das uns folgte corona boreae nimm die
schlange
nimm „himmel“ sag wer du bist weil du warst
kähne
tauchen türme leuchten gib mir norden so
schnell
so langsam das licht das als seil uns wirft und
schwärme
von krähen rufen im wald mit den düften steigen sie
auf
das ist das wasser am abend, korken, krone
lumen
lumen
er, hier

was still little a flat frog with an eye
at one side
the eye that followed us corona boreae take the
snake
take "sky" say who you are because you've been
boats
diving towers lights give me the north so
fast
so slow the light like a rope throwing us and
flocks
of crows call in the forest and rise with the
fragrances
that's the water in the evening, corks, crown
lumen
lumen
him, here

synger med fuld styrke

zu Ruth Berlau and Bert Brecht

BB:
schlamassel schlawiner

august 1933
nach dem hauskauf am skovsbostrand

‚friedlich' ‚idyllisch' was wehten
die dannebrogs wie zungen so
lang auf *flygende asfalt* wildfarben
gelb schlugen pflaumen aufs
dach. bus stop rantzausmindevej.
still nebenan, scharf, die halme
des geschnittenen felds, trat
man hinein, warf es batz
warf schlamm. jemand sagte
grau. jemand sagte schlamassel
sagte irdische farbe schlechthin, dein
grauseidenes hemd, bb, sagte
schlamassel-schlawiner, du. fast
sahen in diesem augenblick die hügel
bayrisch aus. scharf und geschnitten
und still. schlawiner? ein anderes wort
schwang, b und i und anfang und
ende des alphabets. allein, die
buchtung des busses stand
voller nesseln, voll licht.

klang deswegen das keckern
der rebhühner so unüberhörbar
sjov, so keck?

vogel am sund

synger med fuld styrke

on Ruth Berlau and Bert Brecht

BB:

schlemozzle slyboots

august 1933
after buying the house at skovsbostrand

'tranquil' 'idyllic' how lingual
the dannebrogs fluttered how
long on *flygende asphalt* russet
yellow plums dunting on the roof.
the rantzausmindevej bus stop.
quiet next door, sharp the stubble
in the cut field, if you trod in
it threw up slutch
slung mud. someone said
grey. someone said schlemozzle
said the very colour of earth, your
grey silk shirt, bb, said
schlemozzle-slyboots, you. just
then the hills almost looked
Bavarian. sharp-cut and
still. slyboots? another word
lingered, b and i and the first and
last of the alphabet.* only, the
bus-bay was
full of nettles, full of light.

was that why the cackling
partridges sounded so insistently
sjov, so cocky?

bird by the sound

ohne schiff, ohne post
gewickelt um einen irren geschmack
körper bb (bazi bert)
                    inständiger ruf

BB:
auf lauer gelagert

skovsbostrand 8, sommer 1937

... wespen krabbeln an
benutzten gläsern hinauf summen
während sie ertrinken
in den neigen von apfelwein

sonst wo war es bier wo man
schlucken muss und das herz „rast" im zimmer
wie man sagte sonst wo
zuhaus, als wär es von allen träumen

— geräumt türen vier vielleicht fünf
weiße segel kabbelnd überm
sund, ist's ein hals, eng, die
hölzer des daches wie ruder die messer

gekreuzt. warum an ein bild glauben an
ein anderes nicht? im birnen- im wespen-
duft, wepsen wie man sonst
wo sagt, angesessen, mit

heimatschein. stock, hier trocknender
fisch, erinnerst du dich, einmal

sans ship, sans post
twisted round a crazy taste
body bb (bazi bert)
imploring cry

**bazi*: (Bavarian): scamp, scoundrel

BB:
laid-in on the look-out

skovsbostrand 8, summer 1937

… wasps crawl
up the used glasses and hum
while going under
in the dregs of apple wine

elsewhere it was beer where you
had to swallow and your heart "raced" round
the room as the people said elsewhere
at home, as if all its dreams

— broomed now doors four perhaps five
white sails crawling across
the sound, is it a neck, narrow
the spars of the roof like oars knives

crossed. why believe in one image not
in another? in the pear scent
in scent of wasps, *wapses* as
people said someplace else, stuck-at-homes

with their native proof. stock, here drying
fish, do you remember once

warf jemand jenes
fehlende erste wort verlangendes

summen zu dir ins gras für sekunden
süß in der neige das fremde „was hieße
zu bleiben?“ und nachts
wach nicht sich sagen zu müssen es ist

stroh nur stroh das dich bedeckt das
über dir krabbelt mit dem dänischen
                                        wind

RB:
kopenhagen, mein käuflicher garten

sommer 1937

und sie maßen mir zu
                    vielleicht auch gaben
diese tafel mit nägeln gespickt
dort hingen die lettern metallisch
groß wie singbar
die texte wind nahm sie
                    aus den segeln
lange her, eines eingerollt
schlief.
          da wurde das wasser
im strudel der schrauben so schwarz
glatt, hellgrün dann, trieben
im dunkel teilchen
und lief
          der schraube nach
jene schaumige welle wie

somebody threw
that missing first word a yearning

humming to you in the grass for seconds
sweet in the dregs was the foreign "what
would it mean to stay?" and at night
awake not having to tell yourself it's

thatch just thatch that covers you
scuttling above you with the danish
                                        wind

RB:
copenhagen, my garden
for sale

summer 1937

and they allotted to me
        or gifted perhaps
this board all studded with nails
its letters hanging metallic
and large singable too
the texts wind took them
        out of the sails
long ago, one of them curled up
slept.
    then in the whirl of
propellers the water turned so black
smooth, then to bright green, particles
drifting in darkness
and running
    after the propeller
that foamy wave like

            eine hand
die sich überschlagend
                        wiederkam
lebendiger tüll, ophelia-
gerät.

            so unwurm die
lettern, ein vorhang im
wind
            decken lagen vor
der bibliothek steckten
zwei mädchen die
köpfe zusammen und
das wort „kommen“ in
deiner sprache saugte
silben an wie wolken
den himmel „ein“ „vor“
und „aus“ wollten
über uns
sein lebendig
kalter, die maschinen
            umschraubender, mit
            sich selbst vergessen
                    spielender schaum

BB:
im wald von tåsinge, allein/
wo es zu regnen begann

november 1938

stieg den hügel alter schimmernder buchen
hinauf durch tiefes laub sehr weichen boden
den hügel steil hinan einmal waren wir hier
du von den zu kleinen inseln, vom hascherl-land

a hand
curled back
on itself
living tulle, ophelia-
gear.

so un-wormling those
letters, a curtain in the
wind
rugs lay out
in front of the library
two girls putting
their heads together and
the word for "come" in
your language sucked
syllables in like clouds
the sky "up" "to"
and "through" wanted
to be
above us
cold and alive that screw-
whirling self-failing
frolicking foam

BB: in the wood of tåsinge, alone/ where it started to rain

november 1938

climbed the rise of ancient gleaming beeches
through the heaps of leaves the ground
so soft and steep the hill, we were here once
you from islands too small, blown in

angeweht ich. in den bäumen hauste
ein riesenschwarm krähen auch sie stiegen
dicke fette krähen aufgeregt auf, ich
rutschte fast den hang wieder hinab. oben
dann sträucher dornen ein dicklich weißgelbes
feld das von nebel schwamm. abwärts
wie beim skifahren zu ... zuhaus ... die
erleuchteten gestänge der büsche, das hangeln
daran. unten wiederholte sich das feld, drei
kämpfende fasane darin. der wald schien voller
federvieh es gluckste und rief und die bäume
etwa 200 die silbern glatten senkrechten knorpel
gestreckt standen im nebel als ein wesen da
und schoben voran als wäre in einen film ich
geraten in ein stück dänischer angst. es regnete
und war die grenze zwischen zwei wolken
sie hießen exil und zweites exil und ich hörte
dem unsichtbaren aufs butterbrot des buchenlaubs
geschmiert, hasch hush die fähren fahren
im wald

RB:
svendborger lied

sommer 1939

kleiner sechsarmiger lautsprecher
die stockrose am haus ...

das julischiff zieht vorüber
lautlos, zwei große segel, drei kleine
rettungsboot strahlend weiß
schaukelst überm sund

from rabbit-land me. roosting in the trees
was this enormous flock of crows they too
great fat crows climbed in alarm, i
almost slipped back down the slope. on top
then bushes thorns a pasty pale white
field awash with mist. going down
was like skiing back … back home … those
shining branches in the wood, swinging on
them. the field below repeated itself, three
pheasants a-sparring. the woods seemed full
of fowl of gurgles calls and the trees
some 200, their silvery-smooth gristle
erect and taut in the mist a single being
surging forward as if i'd stepped into
some film some slice of danish angst. it rained
and this was the border between two clouds
called exile one and exile two and i heard,
the invisible made as plain as beech
leaves, snatch hush the ferries leaving
in the wood

RB:
svendborg song

summer 1939

little six-armed loudspeaker
hollyhock by the house …

july's ship is passing
silently by, two sails big, three small
lifeboat gleaming white
you sway over the sound

kleiner sechsarmiger lautsprecher
die stockrose am haus …

das schiff zog vorüber
zwei große segel, drei kleine
schwarzweiß sein körper
glich unserem text

das einzige rettungsboot
hing am ende auch
schlugen die wellen
als wollten sie fort

kleiner zweiarmiger laut
stock, rose, am haus.

BB:
bus stop twenty-fifth street santa monica

herbst 1942

was immer schon da war wird deutlich wenn
er an einer bushaltestelle steht in hustenmuster
gehüllt, die fremden straßenlichter steil. wie stumm sie
einwärtsschaut, die mutterhaut, das musenmuster, die mutter
mut nur mut. amerikanischer nervenschwarm (frau nebenan)
lässt familienbatterien an ihn denken. sie feuern ihn englisch
anzufangen etwa als *angel*-fangen (weihnachtssport?) doch
die mitgeführte samenschachtel „sentiment“ (ach bua!
ach komm, ach sperr dich nicht). das sind die
gliederlieder
ja, jede geste jedes wir-zu-zweit (bua bua)
vorab mit sprache eingerüstet und ihre ist’s
und jede reaktion. wie dehnt sich da das zwerch

little six-armed loudspeaker
hollyhock by the house …

the ship has passed us by
two sails big, three small
its body black and white
was like our text

the only lifeboat
hung at the back too
the waves broke
as if to depart

little two-armed sound
holly, hock, by the house.

BB:
bus-stop twenty-fifth street santa monica

autumn 1942

what was always there already shows through when
he stands at a bus-stop wrapped in his inveterate
cough, the foreign streetlamps sheer. how mum
with staring inward, his mother skin, inveterate muse, o *mutter courage* be bold. an american nerve-throb (girl next door)
brings family batteries to bear. they fire him on to pick up
english i.e. angle for angels (an anglo-christmas sport?)
but the seed-box of "sentiment" that comes with him (*ach bua** come on, don't hold back!). such are the
songs of limb and loin
yes every gesture, each just-the-two-of-us (*bua bua*)
already in-scaffolded with language, and hers it is
and every reaction too. how then the diaphragm dilates

wie denkt an wehen er, an blätter, sanftes du, unsprechbar
als geräusch. so bleibt, umarmt er andere, jenes kratzen
tief im hals jenes strecken auch der hand und
ihre ist's er sieht es doch den venenbaum das
rückflussblut, das r das ü das k das l seiner
sprache fell auch innen drin, der heitre
speichel, zarte schlag ……
your ticket please, Sir!
im dunklen bus die scheiben getönt geduckt
er kramt die hand wird alt vom himmel hängt
ein langer nerv der zuckt die angel muttersprache
(er der kleine köder dran) vom himmel in berlin

RB:
herrzange
berlin, charitéstraße 3, herbst 1973

hat eine zuviel b im schrank
batikrock blazer gar eine boa
zum abschlecken einen mit
grünem fell hinter den ohren
augen wie windleuchten
ja, so einen hund! so einen
vielfachstecker dildospieler
der jagt übern stuck der exile
der helfenden hände (schwan
treibt im wasser, sie werden wohl
weiblich sie werden wohl
leder gewesen sein) selbst die
kronen sind teuer hasst
einen b du im schrank
die herzangst das flattern der
hosen gewichsten duke

and how he thinks of wafting, leaves, soft you, unutterable
as a sound. thus remains when he embraces others that itch
deep in his throat, with the hand stretching too it's
hers it is he sees that tree of veins the
backflow of her blood, the *r* the *ü* the *k* the *l* of his
furry language-self and inside too, the spittle
blithe, the tender beat of ......

your ticket please sir!

in the gloomy bus behind tinted glass ducked down
he rummages his pockets his hand grows old and
from above a twitching nerve his angling mother-tongue
(with him its tiny bit of bait) dangles from berlin's sky

* *bua*: Bavarian: boy, *laddie*.

RB:
heart-clawer

berlin, charitéstraße 3, autumn 1973

if in your wardrobe you have too much b
batik skirt and blazer even a boa
to lick of the type that displays
a shock of green fur between
the ears his eyes like storm lamps
yes, a really dirty dog! a
multiple-plug dildo merchant
racing through the stuccoed exiles
of our helping hands (swan
adrift on the waves, they
had to be female, of course, had
to be leather) even the
crowns are expensive if you've
a b in your wardrobe to hate
the anguished heart the flapping
trousers the waxed duke: the way

wie er da sitzt, bronze, faltige
büste (die tausendundvierte – eine
mehr als don juan) steuert noch
immer mit der fernbedienung
matchboxsteyr über den strand
immer wieder die küste, die küste
die kunst.

fuck. es habe erdig
gerochen das hemd
silbern (wie ruhm) (wie
rufe) das blutige rutschen
später in ihrer hand

he sits there, bronze, a wrinkly
bust (the thousand and fourth – one
more than don juan) still at it
with his remote control
matchbox steyr across the beach
coasts forever and again, the coast
his art.

            fuck. so it smelled
earthy that shirt
silvery (like fame) (like
a calling) the bloody slip-slide
later in her hand

dämmerung

im zug hörte ich sie sagen
sie habe nun ein neues lieblingsstück
nathan der weise. blonde dünne haare
ein doppelkinn, jugendspeck. vielleicht
aber auch etwas das aufgeflogen war
auf der suche nach einem zuhause und sich
vorläufig festsetzte in diesem ring ich
dachte an lessing wie er von seiner bibliothek
fast jeden abend nach braunschweig lief
12 kilometer geradeaus, den wald gab es
damals schon. klamm? und er trank
trank bis er nicht mehr konnte spielte
bis er verlor alles verloren hatte, blieb
lief die anderen nächte 12 kilometer durch
dunkelheit und das stehen der bäume. knackende
zweige. glühwürmchen schleppten stille ins
gras. aufklärung, licht? die himmelshunde
rannten so sehr. es winselte nichts. so sagte er
sich ist die dämmerung in meinem eigenen garten.
so bin ich durchflochten mit mir wie der wald

twilight

in the train i heard her say
she had a new favourite play
nathan the wise. thin blonde hair
a double-chin, baby fat. perhaps
too something that had come to light
when searching for a home and which
for now had settled on this ring. i
thought of lessing and how he walked
on most evenings from his library to braunschweig
12 kilometres as the crow flies, the forest
was already there. damp? and he drank
drank until he was full played
until he had lost had lost all, stayed
on the other nights walked 12 kilometres through
darkness and towering trees. cracking
twigs. fireflies drew stillness into
the grass. enlightenment, light? the celestial dogs
ran so fast. no whining here. this he told
himself is how the twilight is in my own garden.
thus like the forest i am entwined with myself

aufgabe, gabe

ich gehe unbehelligt durch den park
du hingegen wirst erwischt. sich gleitend
zu bewegen ohne anzuecken an das
was unsinnigerweise verboten ist
kann angst in mut verwandeln
und das zischen des schwans endet in der
luft. nur ein schluckender schwan
ist ein friedlicher schwan und braucht
nicht monogam
im nest zu sitzen plusternd in den gezeiten
im gezettel im mond der als gelbe blume
nirgends hängt als im auge eines unglücklichen
schwans. welche form nimmt
er an wenn du ihn denkst? die gabe
des schwans ist seine unschmeckbarkeit
und die verweigerung von blau. durch
dessen frequenz ein schwan
zum platzen gebracht werden kann
wie jener in der schule der angeblich aus
venedig tatsächlich einfaches glas sofort
barst. so auch menschen
bestrahlt mit eigenfrequenz in schalltotem
raum. auf einem seil brauchst du dafür nicht
zu gehen. oder denke an den schwamm.
verurteilten die man
mochte auf den kopf gelegt dass der strom
schneller in den körper fand. anderen
brutzelte der skalp. das wusste jeder.
so gelb sind nun die narzissen.

(sub)mission, gift

        i pass through the park undetected
you however get caught. to glide
through it without offence when something
is nonsensically forbidden
        can transform fear into courage
and the hissing of the swan expires in thin
air. only a swallowing swan
is a peaceful swan and need not
        sit monogamously
on the nest ruffling its feathers in the tide
in the litter in the moon which like a yellow flower
hangs nowhere if not in the eye of the unhappy
        swan. what form does it take
when you think of it? the swan's
gift is its untasteability
and refusal of blue. whose
        frequency can be used to make
a swan explode
like the one at school that was meant to be from
venice but was actually ordinary glass and immediately
burst. like people
exposed to natural frequency in a soundproof
room. it's not exactly like walking
on a tight-rope. or think of the sponge.
        placed on the heads
of the condemned you liked so the current
could enter their bodies more quickly. the others'
scalps fried. everyone knew that.
        that's how yellow daffodils are

anthropogen gestörter wuchsplatz

ab
und zu entspringen dem frühling: ent-
dem frühlingsgrünen krokusspringen
forsythienblühen in den wald. teilchen
im wald in der schonung inne – die sich
entrollenden farne die seile die von bäumen
ins licht frühlingsbodenlicht der moose
mit den winzigsten blüten die unsichtbaren
seile die durch die luft insektenwege sich
um eine hüfte schulter zu bündeln was
entsprang das *forsythienpony*
zufällig im krokuslicht ruderalflora sich
jung jünger daherträumendes ich

später frühling
will sagen dümmliche
füllung: später spurt

will „ich“ sagen: wiederholung
ist güte

anthropogenically disturbed growth area

off
and on stem from the spring: out
of spring green crocus stems
forsythia blooms into the woods. particles
in the wood poise in the clearing – the ferns
unfurling strings from trees into light
the spring-floor light of mosses with
minutest blossoms the invisible
strands through the air the paths of insects
gathering to shape a hip shoulder what
sprang out was the *forsythia pony*
chanced on in crocus-light ruderal flora
an 'i' dreaming itself young younger

late spring
meant to say silly
filling: late spurt

meant to say "i": repetition
is kindness

gründung der linguistik

am fort der maidan wie „mädchen“ wie
aber kam es zu „girl“. man macht sternchen
nun für das was nie war nie gewesen sein
darf die unter-über-sprache das segensreich
– der briten in indien, traum unterm kuckuck-
baum. salziges weiches sanskrit. man sagt
mister williams, die wände im fort sind
dünn wie ein zahn. die wurzeln der banjans
das schwanken der luft. man kann ein effekt
oder nur ein ziegenhauch sein. nun
also die mischung, die sprays der kämpfer
so fremd: das angeglichene gesicht. silber-
getriebene elefanten eine maus die den
kopf für pillen nach unten klappt. weit draußen
der friedhof der briten. orangegefärbte
hunde heulen die straßen herbei

founding of linguistics

at the fort on the maidan like 'maiden' but
how did 'girl' come about. they use asterisks
now for what never was is never allowed to have
been the under-over-language the blessed empire
– of the british in india, dreaming under the cuckoo-
tree. salty-soft sanskrit. they say
mister williams, the walls in the fort are
thin as a tooth. the roots of the banjans
the swaying air. you can be an effect
or just a whiff of goat. so now
for the mix, the sprays of the combatants
so strange: their matching faces. elephants
wrought in silver a mouse whose head
flips open for pills. further out
the burial ground of the british. orange-
coloured dogs howl for the streets

subsong

2014

subsong

2014

pangen

(sie spicht kein r)

goß soll es sein das wanden de augen: mein licht benn auf sie
summt sie nickt scheit sieht denkt sie ist das stenlein mischt
und findet weda sich noch uns die günde sind ein matsch
am gummistiefeland blatt patt die ada da de baum „die elsta
fliegt“ schwazweiß de „mond de auch“ wo ist de wald?
die katze unsichtba wikklich sitzt auf de hand da daußen wo
da gang bis es bicht da kug nicht schon und weiß das
baune auge seine heitekeit wenn wie vasteckt sich
was sie .... (ist)

glitt-e-ing

(she doesn't ponounce r)

enomous must be the wandaing eye: shine bight my light she
hums she nods sceams steahs thinks she's a little stah mixes
up and finds neithah hehself noh us the easons ah all mush
on the ubba-boot leaf stuck theah paat of the tee „the coh
flies“ like buhds but „moon ides on dahk“ wheah is the fo-est?
the cat seecetly eal sits on its hand out thea whea it
luhkt and cept so long till not behking the jug and does heh
bown eye know its bightnesss when she hides
what she .... (is)

paprika mamrika

seit drei tagen kann sie das r und
wie sagte sie „paprika“ nach der kita
„mamrika“ wir lachten liefen riefen
ros: fahrradkringer kaufen zur berohnung
währte sie statt rosa rirryfee eine braue
mit maus danach saßen wir im café
sie aß cheesecake wir spierten „große“
sprich machten konversation unter
schaukernden pratanen war sie doch im theater
der rote drache mit den nicht mehl
glünen augen … und erzährte von feuer
und schreichen, herrrich war
das reben in diesem herbst

paprika mamrika

she's been saying r for three days and
how did she say "paprika" after nursery
"mamrika" we raughed ran yerred
rets go: to buy her a bike-berr as a reward
instead of a pink riry fairy she picked a brue
one with a mouse then we sat in a café
she had cheesecake we prayed "big girs"
that is did conversation under prane
trees and forring reafs for wasn't her rore
in the pray the led dlagon whose eyes were no
ronger gleen … and tord me of fire
and srithering, how wonderfur
rife turned this forr

wölf

ein graues kind langhaarig dunkel das braune gesicht weiß verschmiert
klein zart in weiter kleidung einem grauen fleece grauen hosen
festen schuhen ein wolfskind, in seiner art breitschultrig
die paar stufen des busses hinunter kleines wesen noch
nach drei tagen kitafahrt nach schaf riechend erde esel
wie sprachlos in sich mit wildem hetzendem blick
kam sie für sekunden sekunden fremd auf mich zu
die stufen des busses paar stufen eine welt herab
nach drei tagen so fremd. wir mussten erst wieder
suchen wo wir wir waren aufeinanderzufahren
die klebenden oder sich verfugenden ideen
die als arme hände sichtbar waren zwischen uns
als ich sie, sie auf dem arm tragend, weiter berührte
sagte sie „au“ als hätte ich einen bart im gesicht
als hätte mein wölfischer bart sie gestreift
mein wölfischer blick

ich hatte so lange gewartet
ich strich

wolfy

a grey child long-haired dark her brown face smeared white
small delicate in loose clothing a grey fleecy grey trousers
sturdy shoes a wolf-child, broad-shouldered in her way
coming down the few steps from the bus little thing still
after three day's kindergarten trip smelling of sheep donkey earth
as if speechless self-contained with wild questing gaze
for seconds seconds strange coming towards me
down the steps of the bus a few steps a world
after three days so strange. we needed first to
find out where our we was to move towards
each other those gluing or joining ideas
visible between us as arms and hands
when i, carrying her in my arms, kept touching her
she said "ow" as if i'd grown a beard
as if my wolfish beard had brushed her
my wolfish gaze

i'd been waiting so long
i prowled

taumel der trennung

morgens vor dem spiegel **ich**
träumend denk und **dreh**
um dich **da** wird die kehle
mir **noch** eng denn du sagst
durch welches öhr willst du
dass ich schlüpf um dich **da**
rauszudrehen sage **ich** hat
mir gerade **noch** gefehlt
dass **durch** zu vieler spiegel
dreh ich dich nirgends mehr
versteh der an der gläser **dreh**
glaubt er säh wie **ich** mir uns
als wir gedacht **da**rin ein du das
drückt und **noch** mit schaum
durch die zähne zu mir spricht
was musst du wütend sein **da**bei
obwohl, welch blitz, du **durch** den
spiegel lachst als **dreh**te mich
um dich **noch** immer munter
ich und schaute nie an dir
                                        vorbei

separation spin

morning at the mirror musing **i'm**
pondering how i'm **going**
round and **round** you when you
whisper **the** spell you think will
bend my ear to tell you the eye
of the needle to enter to get **round**
me winkle me out **the** hell with
that i choke light **bend**s and i
can see **i'm** only flailing
going nowhere just a blur
of mirrors where you glimpse **the**
whirl of us at every **bend**
miss that you **i'm** thinking's
you that's **going** to hurt and
spin a**round** to spit your
rage in the mirror i **round** on
this laughing you **i'm** sure
thinks i'm **going** to blithely
keep **the** circles turning
bending to please not faced
away

sich verstecken

als haughty horse (fremdsprache) schwankend
und steif leider nicht im taxi sondern in meinem
haus schon eingezogen zog mein mann andere frauen
aus. das zimmer verkrustete in fasrige wände dass man
nicht gehen könne dass man fliegen müsse die anderen
(fliehen) hatten ein telefon mit ihm verschmolzen da
wurde in der dunkelheit des allgemeinen kletterns ich
der prinz der den blick nicht ertrug, gewickelt
in eines fleck-gefickten ponys fell. zeige dir
sagte mein mann die vielfalt deiner eigenen
inneren fallen hyperreal bist du die wand
der sessel die schlange und ebeneben das seelchen
wie es wieder nur weißlich, made mädlein
den eigenen großen gequollenen augen über
den flokati folgt. willst du's wirklich erhämmern?
da dachte ich an das alte maulwurfspiel, man
schlug die dunklen hügel ein der andere steuerte
die cd im computer. es ging um blindes
das zurückgedrückt in seine höhle fast erstickt
doch noch immer zärtlich rudernd die erde
einmal ganz zu umkriechen versucht

hiding

as a *haughty horse* (foreign tongue) swaying
and stiff regrettably not in the taxi but already
moved into my house my husband undressed other
women. the room scabbed up with fibrous walls so
you couldn't walk would have to fly the others
(fleeing) had him fused to their phones when
in the dark of this all-out scrabbling i became
the prince who could not stand the sight wrapped
in a fuck-flecked pony's coat. i'll show you
said my husband the variety of your own
inward traps you hyper-really are the wall
the chair the snake and yet-yet again the snow
flake the whitish bit of girlish grime trailing
its big own swollen eyes across the shaggy
deep-pile. really? trying to hammer it in?
made me think of that mole game where you had
to bash down black hills, with the other person
controlling the computer. fighting about a blind
thing forced back into its hole and practically
suffocating while still rowing tenderly
it strove to crawl right round the earth

sachlicher schlich

„Es war die Nachtigall!“
„Die Lerche war's!“
Ach

zum regal: wie man
ein buch entnimmt aufschlägt liest bis rötlich
wie lungenschlotz des morgens erste kralle
himmelsturm schleierlich der alte minnesong
das kraulen jener luft mit reiher kranich federzug
bestückt november blumig treibt lichter auf
zieh stulpen an gib fingerspiel dem dämmerlicht
am fensterblech ein wespenpaar sie dick
er klein auf ihrem rücken festgetäut die ficken
was aus dauernd lang tausend wespen stiche
nächstes jahr. rasch man hat doch auch
geräusch (mädchen dame hirn gestirn)
wie fliegt beim kamera klick das gebilde
auf das trennt sich nicht das brummt.
kurz denkt man noch das gelbe blatt das
rote blatt des treidelns schlich der sonne
kurzer stich das segeln fallen eisig sein

sober slink

'It was the nightingale!'
'It was the lark!'
Oh

to the shelves: the way
you take down a book and read till rosy
as sludge from a lung the dawn's first talon
raids the hazy heavens – the old morning song
ruffling a sky that's decked with plume strokes
of heron crane a bloomy november whips up lights
pull on your wrist warmers finger-play the twilight
on the window sill a pair of wasps her plump
him slighter strapped to her back they're fucking
which at that rate's a thousand wasp stings
for the coming year. but quick you feel
a tumult too (maid ma'am brain star)
the way their duo flies up at the camera's
click they're undivided still they're all abuzz.
a flash of thought: the yellow leaf the
leaf in red your slinking shuffle the sun's
short stab the sailing falling being ice

wulkan

(lwiw – wrocław – berlin)

weißt du wie es ist wenn man
schleudert (das fallende laub) fragte er
mit weicher polnischer ruhe:
wulkan.

die lage der kanten das porzellan
sagte er alle gegenstände des hauses
erinnerten an eigene bedürfnisse: fotos
von kindstaufen eine blau träumende
kommode mit stolzierendem emaillepfau
der wein vom hochzeitsjahr
der anderen.
noch warm ihre deutschen lippen
noch auf den gläsern
der spüle. wir schämten
uns nicht des nehmens
des sehens wohl. so
kamen wir
nicht an.
wulkan.
lebensbild
hergebracht. gemälde
aller schatten an der wand
schichten aus mensch gestapelt
fruchtbar heiß, erstarrt. im eigenen
dreißig jahre auf gepackten koffern
gesessen: was fliehen
in geflohenes
heißt.
zersägten
das bett die anderen

wulkan

(polish: volcano)

(lviv – wrocław – berlin)

do you know what it's like when you
spin (the falling leaves) he asks
with gentle polish calm:
wulkan.

the lay of the edges the porcelain
all the things in the house he said
put them in mind of their own needs: photos
of christenings, the blue dream
of a dresser with prancing enamel peacock
the wine from the wedding year –
theirs that is.
the warmth still of their german lips
on the glasses
by the sink. we were
ashamed not of taking
but of looking. that
wasn't the way we got on.
wulkan.
figure for life
passed on. tableau
of all the shadows on the wall
layers of the human piling up
prolific and hot, frozen. sitting
on packed bags in your own place
for 30 years: fleeing
to what others
have fled.

they sawed up
the bed the others

um zu heizen den einen geretteten
sack das holzbein des toten sohns.
ich kann ihre hände sehen vater
großvater großmutter ihre nägel
sie hatten nicht alles verloren
fast noch alle teile des körpers
bei sich noch etwas seele –
vielleicht

man legt sich nieder und liebt sich
in europäischem gras. ein turm
ragt auf, aus eisen und rekonstruktion
das ist normal. eine straßenbahn
fährt. das herz wulkan
weich gegen die wände
huft in einem brüchigen
polnischen stall.

for fuel the only salvaged
sack the wooden leg of a dead son.
i can see their hands, father
grandfather grandmother their nails
they had not lost everything
had kept almost all their body parts
kept something of the soul –
perhaps

people lying down and making love
on european grass. a tower
rises, all iron and reconstruction
that is the norm. a tram
passes. the heart wulkan
soft against the walls
beats its hooves in a ramshackle
polish stable.

regen mit rüskensnepp

am boden:
tick-a tick
blick-blick-blick

schlickgrau
schiefergrau: himmel
verhalftert glänzender schorf
strunk der baum. wäre sie nicht
zu breit verkröche sie sich darin
keine drei meter der weg hinter ihr
gleitenden dicht klebenden
wassers wand entrückt auch
was vor ihr liegt

gedaunt: deckung duckung tarn
sanftmut ins gefieder gestreift
in blase stiller wirklichkeit bekassine
rüschenschwänzchen erscheint
saugschnabel schlammgetaucht kommt
lautlos auf der regen über sand ist
was sie hört sie selbst das knirschen
der ölhaut der pelerine reiben
kaum dreht sie den kopf

hintereinander landein kurzer
frauenfaden waagrecht zwischen
regenfäden, himmellang
                    bewegen-gesunden
das schaukeln des körpers als teil
sich einer uralten schweigsamen horde
gefühlt der buhnen kriegerköpfe
tangbärte wehend im griff der see
sich öffnenden see

rain with mire snite

on the ground:
tick-a tick
keek-keek-keek

silt-grey
slate-grey: sky-
strapped gleaming scurf-
stump the tree were she not
so broad she'd hole up there
barely three yards behind her the path
erased by the sliding tightly clinging
water's wall everything
in front of her too

downy: cover-cowering disguise
softness streaked into plumage
in her bubble of hushed realness snipe
fantail going up
beak sunk deep into mud sucks comes
up silently rain on sand is
what she hears herself the scrunching
of her oilskin her cape's rasping
barely turns her head

one behind the other inland
the short thread of women crosses
between rain-threads, sky-long
        exercise-healing
in the swaying of their bodies feel
part of an ancient silent horde
the groyne's warrior-heads
weed-beards wafting in the sea's hand
the opening sea

peitscht wasser eine möwe
ihr über den scheitel schier
was hat eine möwe für
ein herz. meergras geknäult
ihres fliegt quer zum strand
weiße krebse die gischtscheren
sehnsüchtig zur brandung
gestreckt. sonne, pelerine
platzendes rot.

aus nichts
spiegeln die wolken
ein meer zusätzlicher moleküle
aufs meer. sie steht zwischen
den abermals senkrecht
groß fallenden tropfen.
warm, gelöst wie der regen
gleiten ihr die federn
vom leib

water whips a gull
streams down her parting
what kind of heart does a seagull
have a bundle of sea-wrack
hers flies crosswise to the beach
white crabs their foam scissors
stretching longingly
for the surf. sun a cape
bursting red.

out of nowhere
the clouds mirror
a sea of additional molecules
onto the sea. she stands
among the large drops
falling vertically again.
warm, loosed like the rain
the feathers slip
from her body

aufersteh, schnee

zaunkönig

wit wit wit
scheun wedder hüt
und dat frrrreujoorrrrrr
is nich mehr wit

klümpchen unterschiedlichen
umfangs, unterschiedlichen streichs
– klein, pluderig wie *im herbst*
erst geschlüpft flogen auf – landeten
schritts – eins ums andre
in unberührten schnee
hint
über sich warf
gespreizten flügels
wit

bleib liegen
bleib bleib

rücken
kuhle-um-kuhle
zitterten kicherten
bis in die spitzen
sechs sieben

wit
bleib bleib

am häuschensockel krallenfries
aus eis. grünäugige mörderin
schneescheu scharf auf
schrei im haus *tschill tschill*
die bäuchin schlief.

resurrectio, snow

wren (a fence kinglet)

whit whit twit
gt wedder innit
ndits sprrrrrrrrring
innabit

clumplets of differing
girth, of differing dab
– small, puffed as if *hatched*
only this autumn flew up – landed
astride – one by one
in the untouched snow
          top topp-
ling over backwards
     wings splayed
     whit

sit tight
sit tight

backs
hollow-by-hollow
a-tremble a-giggle
to the roots
six seven

     whit
sit sit

on the house-plinth a claw-frieze
of ice. the green-eyed murderer
snow-shy lusts
for squeals indoors *tchill-tchill*
pouchy-pouch dosed.

sah sie nicht auffliegen. weiß
umgeben von schattenweiß
blieben im schnee ihre kuhlen
gräber, doch leer, ostern
doch scherz: sieben
auf einen mut.

sanken langsam
die risse tauten zu
boden ins gras. frühling
herrisch durchnässt
grünäugig fast. nie
kehrten die könige zurück
nicht wirklich nicht wie
sie waren: kuhle-um-kuhle

glitzernde zucker
aus licht

did not see them fly up white
surrounded by shadow-white
their hollows left in the snow
graves, but empty, easter
but joke: seven
of one pluck.

subsided slowly
the gouges melting
earthward into the grass. springtime
oppressively sodden
green-eyed almost. never
again did the kinglets return
not really not like
they were then: hollow-for-hollow

twinkling twitchers
of light

wanderfalke

> „Am besten betritt und verlässt man jeden Tag zur selben Zeit die Felder und beschwichtigt das Wilde im Falken mit Verhaltensritualen." —J.A. Baker

jeden mittag
stürze ins scherbenfeld
der stunde zu der ich schlüpfte
der eihaut dichte zerbrach die dichte
des windes der nager geschrei. meine
eltern verlor (wisst ihr wie wenige
wir) eine fremde kam fütterte
lehrte mich

jeden mittag
stürze ins scherbenfeld
die karrees der obstgärten
hecken der äcker weißdorn
rotdorn knirschend das weiß
vergiftete gras die ragenden
schollen (wie wenige wir)
in 1000 metern höhe
          zerscherbten geflügelten
                    gesichts

rausche terzel
          bürzel schiefer
auf speed durch die tiefen
lagunen des himmels
                    selbstwerfer
von den kämmen der zirrus
der dickrindigen erdenluft
messer und blatt (die sonne
im rücken, gewiss)

peregrine

> "Enter and leave the same fields at the same time each day, soothe the hawk from its wildness by a ritual of behaviour as invariable as its own." —J.A. Baker

at noon each day
stooping over the shardfield
of the hour i hatched the egg
sac's density burst by the taut sheath
of the wind the rodent's scream. lost
my parents (you know how few
we) a stranger came fed
instructed me

at noon each day
stooping over the shardfield
the squares of orchards
hedges fields whitethorn
pinkthorn crunching the white
poisoned grass the jutting
clods (how few we)
at 3000 feet
      of shatter-winged
                face

tercel rush
      dorsal-slated
speeding through the deep
lagoons of the heavens
            self-flinger
from the crests of the cirrus
from the thick-barked earth-air
ripper and blade (out of
the sun, sure)

schmettere
zu boden
          sehne saum strich
welt aus woge welle
farbe zerstoßenen holzes
versinkendes land

die federn um meine augen
absorbiertes licht. dass
der jäger das gejagte
wird? klemme dich in

deinen vieräugigen kopf
der schnellende flügel
blitzt durch deinen schlaf
schwimmt etwas schlangenhaft
gleitet durch ein gepflügtes
feld. enten rufen
gewiss.

du heischst. über
der mündung suche
flügelhalt in der salzigen
glätte der luft.

dash
to the ground
          sinew seam streak
wave-world surging
colour of pounded wood
sinking land

the feathers round my eyes
absorbed light. so the
hunter may become the
hunted? squeeze into

your four-eyed head
the swooping wing
bolting through your sleep
swimming almost snake-
like gliding through a ploughed
field. ducks call
sure.

you craving. above
the estuary seek
wing-hold in the salt-flushed
sleekness of the air.

pastorale

zwei schneeweiße vögel am ende
des parkplatzes schienen zu balzen
(außer der zeit) kämpften in ihrem winterkleid
perfekt gepasst in ihr leben, dachte, als beute
ich. blechgeruch herbst der scharren jagt
in jeden krallenfuß die letzte nervosität
die unrast fett (stammen vogel-mensch
doch voneinander ab?). mülleimer quollen
über im übrigen war der riesige parkplatz
riesig und leer, ruderale flora, ackerheller
kartoffelrose aus asiatischen jets gesamt.
satt schmatzte die autotür silberblitz fuhr
um glimmer ich die lider kniff. war mit acht
„out of the blue" extrem kurzsichtig geworden
(das bluternährte auge, sein ich) nahsichtig
out of the blue.

rüttler, bagger, grube umsichtig gesiebt
so bauschild, metalle öle (keineswegs
kännchen, kein buch) jahrzehnte gesickert
gepresst. standen sonntag die maschinen
und bäume, einzig die schneeweißen vögel
ließen nicht ab vom programm ihrer gene
verraten, dachte ich, animiert überhell
perfekte schrift auf dem asphaltgrau
der speisekarte *zum falken & fuchs*. ist
nahsichtigkeit evolutionär? lupe die krallte
in jede pore meinen blick alle eingänge
münder sich in alle löcher mich
meiner haut.

pastorale

two snow-white birds at the end
of the parking lot seemed to be courting
(out of season) sparring in a winter plumage
perfectly adapted to their life thought i –
as prey. tin smell autumn a last edginess
surging into every scratcher's claw
restlessness fat (so birds-humans really
stem from each other?). refuse bins
overflowed the huge parking lot otherwise
was huge and empty, ruderal flora, pennycress
rugosa seeded by asian jets.
the car door lip-smacked, silver flashed
i clenched my lids at the glitter. at eight
had become extremely short-sighted "out of the blue"
(the blood-nourished eye, its i) near-sighted
out of the blue.

compactors, diggers, dump sifted with care
said the sign, metals, oils (anything
but cans, no book) seepage for decades
compressed. a sunday, machines and trees
still, only the snow-white birds persisting
in the programme encoded in their genes
betrayed, i thought, vividly blazing
perfect script on the tarmac grey
of the menu at the *falcon & fox*. is
near-sightedness evolutionary? magnifier
clawing my gaze into every pore into orifices
mouths into every hole me
of my skin.

felsbrocken schneidender duft. keine
vogue-slim kein energydrink zum entspannen
hier. rötliches hätte erbeten tröstliches –
gesprenkeltes pony drusen oder drüsen
(unterschied mir wacholder) ich nicht.
flechten sternförmig zart die fetten
vogelpulse rasende morgenluft. unwägbar
sagte das tablet, wer winters
im käfig zeige eine hälfte
richtungsverhalten die andere glatte
stirn. grube zur linken, passiert.
vor mir flogen auf, sanken – zwei
kanister. *schneeweiß*
schneeweiß biozid. der eine
noch mit seinem roten
schnabelverschluss.

frei strich auf
der wind. der jetzt immer bläst
über die gemischten erden der brache
die gifte im versteppenden gras.
                                        niemand
saß da und strickte das betörende
pony. *starlicide starlicide* sang
die luft. zufallsspiel tablet
tick yes, tick no: ist albino
widersinn? denkst du es
leuchtet? die verfallsdaten
konnte ich nicht lesen. nicht
von so verdammt nah.

boulder biting odour. no
vogue-slim no energy drink for relaxation
here. would have asked for something rubicund
comforting – spotted pony druses or daisies
(the difference all juniper to me) not for me.
delicate lichens star-shaped the heavy heart-
beat of the birds a giddy morning air. imponderable
said the tablet who caged
in winter would part show
directional behaviour part placid
brow. pit on the left, past it.
flying up in front of me, sinking – two
canisters. *snow-white*
snow-white biocide. one of them
still with its red
anti-leak beak.

freely wafted
the wind. which now perpetually blows
through the mixed earths of this waste land
the toxins in the withering grass.
                              nobody
sat there knitting the charming
pony. *starlicide starlicide* sang
the air. a tablet game of chance
tick yes tick no: is albino
a nonsense? do you think it
glows? i couldn't read
the use-by dates. not
from so damn close.

berg am laim

komme auf die terrasse von der ich in zwei richtungen
sehen kann zur straße (müllautos, die tonne) und zu dem
kirschbaum dem der garten gehört das haus der uhrichs
nebenan, gelb. bin drei jahre alt vier vielleicht fünf eben
geworden (im winter) älter niemals, nicht hier.

die kirsche ist hoch wie ein baum es nur für kinder sein
kann. kirsche die mir als säugling beschattete das gesicht
auf dem ersten foto das sie wagten aufzunehmen schlafe
ich unter ihren ästen die als freunde ich erinnere und weiß
schatten kommen hierher zurück schwimmen als fische
doppelt, im zimmerglas und im teich.

noch ist niemand krank oder ahnt es nicht niemand
gestorben großvater bückt sich betagt steif über
die gelbe rose am haus. ich weine renne davon als er
sie beschneidet, fühle sie, schlimmer noch fühle
ihn: wie er nicht fühlt.

komme in den garten zurück in dem stumm ich sein durfte
katzen besprühte um zu erfahren wer ich war. sommer früher
sommer mutter zuhause mutter noch nicht so reibend
für mich hausfrau (ihr schimpfen über alle die „arbeiten
gingen“) hat pfannkuchen gebacken wie immer mit butter
– wie ihre mutter

                                   hilflose reime, mit küche bedeckt. sie roch
danach wie etwas anbrennt und nach geriebenem apfel
während vater zurückkommt langen schrittes. wie dünn
und jung er ist kann ich sehen denn ich bin hier
in dem körper von damals mit blitzen

berg am laim

come onto the patio from where i can see in two
directions to the street (rubbish lorries, bin) and to the
cherry tree the garden belongs to the uhrichs' house
next door, yellow. am three four perhaps i've turned
five (in winter) never older, not here.

the cherry's as tall as a tree can only be to
a child. the cherry that shaded my face as a baby
on the first photograph they dared to take, asleep
beneath branches i remember as friends and know
shadows return here as fish swimming
double, in the bowl and in the pond.

no one is ill yet or feels foreboding no one
has died grandfather elderly bends stiffly over
the yellow rose by the house. i cry run away when
he cuts it, feeling it, even worse feeling
him: how he has no feeling.

come back to the garden where i could be silent
spraying cats to discover who i was. summer early
summer mother at home mother not yet so galling
to me hausfrau (railing against those who "took a
job") has made us pancakes as always with butter
– like her own mutter

                    helpless rhymes, kitchen-baked. they made
her smell like something burning and of grated apple
while father returns with long strides. how thin
and young he looks as i can see because i am here
in my then-body in flashes

der erinnerung
aus zellen, die, als hätten sie seelen
eine jede für sich

sich einprägten mein geringes maß. vater, akten
unterm arm, weißes hemd, riecht nach vater nach
zuhausesein auch wenn er mir den kopf abriss
weil ich ihn einer blume abgerissen hatte
denn alles gehörte ihm.

mutter hat angst vor ihm ich auf ihrem arm sehe ihn
als flugzeug das über uns fliegt davon. nur eine tochter
ist echt die andere erinnerung – kehrt mich zurück
in den garten in die flugschneise zu den ersten kirschblüten
und dem teich mit der weide durch den schatten
galoppieren

nie ich selbst nur
hirsche und wolken, katzen
und hasen scheinen sich von oben
und unten aufeinander-
zu-zu-gleichen, seelen der
zellen: was einschreibt
bewahrt

noch ist niemand krank niemand gestorben meine
neue schwester schreit im haus unversehens teilen
wir ein zimmer gelbe rosen klettern über seine äußere
mauer wie ich in sich gefältelt und wild duftend stärker
als alles was gebacken wird oder je gesagt, bin vier
jahre fünf

bekomme zuckerwerk beim bäcker übersetze das lallen
der zu früh geborenen die zu langsam lernt silbe
um silbe schiebe sprache ich an die prachtfinken

of memory
from cells which as if they had souls
each for itself

inscribed my little measure. vater, files
under arm a white shirt smelled of father
of being at home even if he bit my head off
because i had torn one off a flower
for all things belonged to him.

mother fears him while i in her arms see him
as a plane flying over us and away, only one
daughter is real the other memory – sweeping me back
to the garden to the flight path to first cherry blossom
and willow by the pond through which shadows
gallop

never me myself but only
deer and clouds, cats
and hares seeming ever more
alike from above and
below, souls of
cells: whatever encodes
retains

no one is ill yet no one has died my new
sister bawls in the house suddenly we share
a room and yellow roses climb its outer
wall like me infolded and wildly fragrant stronger
than all things baked or ever said, am four
years old five

get iced buns at the baker's translate the babble
of the prematurely born who's a slow learner syllable
for syllable i thrust language at the firefinches

in ihrem käfig, an die fische, vom schwimmen rund.
sitze auf dem dreirad, zu groß schon dafür, schaue
den kirschbaum, den ich liebe.

zu weiß die flugzeuge
darüber in denen ich seither flog.
                    menschen, die ich vermisse
streifen metallisch meine in blitzen
sich faltende stirn

in their cage at the fishes round from swimming.
sit on a tricycle i've already outgrown, looking
at the cherry tree i love.

too white the aeroplanes
above in which i've flown since.
          people i miss
brush metallically my in flashes
wrinkling brow

what is poetry?

putzen staubsaugen rotz abwischen geschürftes knie
bauch streicheln zum einschlafen oder wenn er wehtut
ein bettlied singen vorlesen die beine spreizen empfänglich
und tröstlich sein die wäsche in die trommel stopfen
schamhaare aus dem abfluss fischen zum zehnten mal
den klodeckel schließen die gesamten becher der familie
auf der spülmaschine abgestellt in die maschine räumen
fluchen aber unhörbar an die erziehung des mannes
denken jede erziehung aufgeben sich bücken den hund
füttern mensch ärgere dich nicht spielen wie ein trottel
endlich im bad tür von innen abschließen nach einer minute
riesengeschrei: rotz abputzen marmeladenbrot schmieren
marmeladenbrot vom teppich klauben badeanzüge
auswaschen selbst den ganzen tag nicht rausgekommen
hausschlüssel suchen multi-tasking bewundern
und verachten als mutti-tasking verhören toten vogel
vom fensterbrett schippen sich nicht ekeln ihn
in den garten bringen blick auf den sonnensturm
schmetterlinge das ganze zeug am tümpel (muss
auch endlich saubergemacht werden) libellen
für sekunden die spiegelung
sehen: sich selbst
        halbdämmrig, klein
        ein kind das die weißen
        zähne zeigt, deine zähne

es ist dein körper
du weißt kein besseres wort
        für das, was du siehst, lebendig
        und von dir
        unterschieden
weiß es mehr über dich als dir recht

what is poetry?

cleaning vacuuming wiping snot a scraped knee
tummy-stroking at bedtime or when it's sore singing
lullabies reading stories spreading your legs receptive
and soothing stuff dirty washing in drum fishing
pubic hair out of plughole for umpteenth time closing
toilet lid loading family's entire collection of mugs
left on top of the dishwasher into machine cursing
but inaudibly pondering the upbringing of men
abandoning all upbringing bending to feed dog
playing parcheesi like a numpty at long last locking
oneself in the bathroom but one minute later total
pandemonium: wiping snot spreading jam sandwich
picking jam sandwich out of shag-pile washing
their swimsuits having not set a foot out all day
hunting the house-key admiring then despising
multi-tasking misheard as mummi-tasking shovel
dead bird off window-ledge not finding it icky
carrying it out to the garden taking in the solar storm
butterflies the stuff they've left by the pond (itself
desperately in need of cleaning) dragonflies
for seconds the reflection: yourself
    bleary, small
    a child flashing its
    white teeth, your teeth

it is your body
you have no better word
    for what you see – vital
    and detached
    from yourself
knowing more about you than you

sein kann es sagt: ich liebe
dich tiefer als einen wald

es sagt: dunkel ist das innere des mundes
und alles was denkt

can bear it says: my love
for you is deeper than a forest

it says: dark is the inside of the mouth
and all that thinks

Uncollected

exit erdbeer-klee

Ausgangslage, Auwald Leipzig, 30. April 201

Der Erdbeer-Klee (Trifolium fragiferum) ist eine ausdauernde krautige Pflanze. Die Blattspreite teilt sich kleetypisch in drei, hat man Glück findet man vier. Die Fiederblättchen sind zart mit feingesägtem Rand, die köpfchenförmigen Blütenstände von tiefem Rosa erscheinen zwischen Juni und September im Wald, Schmetterlingsblüte nennt man ihre Form. Sie flügeln hinüber in eine erdbeerartige, leicht rosafarbene Hülsenfrucht, zart behaart, kunstvoll geschuppt, leuchtend erhoben zwischen allem Grün. [https://de.wikipedia.org/wiki/Trifolium_fragiferum]

rundum blühte scharbockskraut graben-
veilchen in den trog des krans gehievt wir ins
sonnengeflecht: die weite des waldes. wipfelgrün
wogenmeer erstsprache lichtsauger überallsprache
chemie die au ein körper aus lücke und wiederholung
tausend einzelwesen gesetzt muster irregel. wald
poetisches system. vögel ohne scheu. erkennen uns
dort oben nicht wieder oder nehmen weil wir stapfer
am grund die krone nicht begreifen als andere uns wahr?
aussterben überbewertet # natur dient. wir jagen
strahlen dürfen das. uns – ich bitte euch – gehört.
bitte, blick um die ecke der berührungslosigkeit.
von seele zu sprechen wage ich nicht. darf ich fragen
wo wir einsilbig werden? über den wipfeln ist ruh?
du spürst den erdwind
wirst teil des bäumischen meers

Stufe 1 (exit *r*)

undum blühte schabockskaut gaben-
veilchen in den tog des kans gehievt wi ins
sonnengeflecht: die weite des waldes. wipfelgün
wogenmee estspache lichtsauge übeallspache

Exit Strawberry Clover

Point of Departure, Floodplain Forest, Leipzig, 30 April 2019

The strawberry clover *(Trifolium fragiferum)* is a herbaceous perennial. The lamina, typically for clover, consists of three leaflets; with luck, four. The pinnate leaflets are delicate and finely serrated. The inflorescence forms a reddish head and appears in forests between June and September. The flowers are described as butterfly-shaped (papilionacious). In time these wing their way to a light pink to become a finely haired, elaborately scaled, strawberry-like legume, tall and bright among the surrounding greenery. [https://en.wikipedia.org/wiki/Trifolium_fragiferum]

all around us pilewort in bloom fen
violet into the tub of the crane us heaved into the
sun's web: the vastness of the forest. treetop-green
billowing ocean first tongue light-sucker overall-language
chemical the floodplain a body of gaps and repetition
a thousand single beings as patterned disorder. forest
a poetic system. unscared birds. not recognizing us
up here or: because we plodders of the ground do not
grasp the canopy perceiving in us another?
extinction overrated # nature serves. we hunt
radiate are entitled. belongs – if you please – to us.
        please, squint around the corner of untouchability.
i dare not speak of the soul. may i ask where we are
turning monosyllabic? over the treetops a hush?
                    you feel the earthly wind
you are part of the tree-fold sea

Stage 1 (exit *r*)

all aound us pilewot in bloom fen
violet into the tub of the cane us heaved into the
sun's web: the vastness of the foest. teetop-geen
billowing ocean fist tongue light-sucke oveall-language

chemie die au ein köpe aus lücke und wiedeholung
tausend einzelwesen gesetzt muste iegel. wald
poetisches system. vögel ohne scheu. ekennen uns
dot oben nicht wiede ode nehmen weil wi stapfe
am gund die kone nicht begeifen als andee uns wah?
aussteben übebewetet # natu dient. wi jagen
stahlen düfen das. uns – ich bitte euch – gehöt.
            bitte, blick um die ecke de beühungslosigkeit.
von seele zu spechen wage ich nicht. daf ich fagen
wo wi einsilbig weden? übe den wipfeln ist uh?
                                    du spüst den edwind
wist teil des bäumischen mees

Stufe 2 (exit e und *n*)

udum blüht schabockskaut gab-
vilch id tog ds kas ghivt wi-is
sogflcht: di wit ds walds. wipflgü
wogm stspach lichtsaug üballspach
chmi di au köp aus lück ud widholug
tausd izl-ws gstzt must igl. wald
potischs systm. vögl oh schu. k'us
dot ob icht wid od hm wil wi stapf
am gud di ko icht b'gif als ad us wah?
ausstb übbwtt # atu dit. wi jag
stahl düf das. us – ich bitt uch – g'höt.
            bitt, blick um di ck d bühugslosigkit.
vo sl zu spch wag ich icht. daf ich fag
wo wi isilbig wd? üb d wipfl ist uh?
                              du spüst dd'wid
wist til ds bäumisch ms

chemical the floodplain a body of gaps and epetition
a thousand single beings as pattened disode. foest
a poetic system. unscaed bids. not ecognizing us
up hee o: because we ploddes of the gound do not
gasp the canopy peceiving in us anothe?
extinction oveated # natue seves. we hunt
adiate ae entitled. belongs – if you please – to us.
        please, squint aound the cone of untouchability.
i dae not speak of the soul. may i ask whee we ae
tuning monosyllabic? ove the teetops is hush?
                        you feel the eathly wind
you ae pat of the tee-fold sea

Stage 2 (exit e and *n*)

all aoud us pilwot i bloom f
violt ito th tub of th ca us havd ito th
su's wb: th vastss of th fost. ttop-g
billowig oca fist togu light-suck ovall-laguag
chmical th floodplai a body of gaps ad ptitio
a thousad sigl bigs as pattd disod. fost
a potic systm. uscad bids. ot cogizig us
up h o: bcaus w plodds of th goud do ot
gasp th caopy pcivig i us aoth?
xtictio ovatd # atu svs. w hut
adiat a titld. blogs – if you plas – to us.
        plas, squit aoud th co of utouchability.
i da ot spak of th soul. may i ask wh w a
tuig moosyllabic? ov th ttops a hush?
                        you fl th athly wid
you a pat of th t-fold sa

Stufe 3 (exit *b, d, l* und *k*)

uum üht schaosaut ga-
vich i tog s as ghivt wi-is
sogfcht: i wit s was. wipfgü
wogm stspach ichtsaug üaspach
chmi i au köp aus ück u wihoug
taus iz-ws gstzt must ig. wa
potischs systm. vög oh schu. us
ot o icht wi o hm wi wi stapf
am gu i ko icht gif as a us wah?
ausst üwtt # atu it. wi jag
stah üf as. us – ich itt uch – g'höt.
          itt, i um i ü-hugs-osig-it.
vo s zu spch wag ich icht. af ich fag
wo wi isiig w? üwipf ist uh?
                              u spüst wi
wist ti s äumisch ms

Stufe 4 (exit s)

uum üht chaoaut ga-
vich i toga ghivt wi-i
ogfcht: i wit wa. wipfgü
wogm tpach ichtaug üapach
chmi i au köp au ück u wihoug
tau iz-wg tzt mutig. wa
potich ytm. vög oh chu. u
ot o icht wi ohm wi wi-tapf
am gu iko icht gifa au wah?
aut üwtt # atu it. wi jag
tah üfa. u – ich itt uch – g'höt.
          itt, i um i ü-hug-oig-it.
vo zu pch wag ich icht. af ich fag
wo wiiig w? üwipf ituh?
                              u püt wi
wit tiäu mich m

Stage 3 (exit *b, d, l* and *k*)

a aou us piwot i oom f
viot ito th tu of th ca us hav ito th
su's w: th vastss of th fost. ttop-g
iowig oca fist togu ight-suc ova-aguag
chmica th foopai a oy of gaps a ptitio
a thousa sig igs as patt iso. fost
a potic systm. usca is. ot cogizig us
up h o: caus w pos of th gou o ot
gasp th caopy pcivig i us aoth?
xtictio ovat # atu svs. w hut
aiat a tit. ogs – if you pas – to us.
        pas, squit aou th co of utouchaiity.
i a ot spa of th sou. may i as wh w a
tuig moosyaic? ov th ttops a hush?
                                you f th athy wi
you a pat of th t-fo sa

Stage 4 (exit *s*)

a aou u piwot i oom f
viot ito th tu of th ca u hav ito th
u' w: th vat of th fot. ttop-g
iowig oca fit togu ight-uc ova-aguag
chmica th foopai a oy of gap a ptitio
a thoua ig ig a patt io. fot
a potic ytm. uca i. ot cogizig u
up h o: cau w po of th gou o ot
gap th caopy pcivig i u aoth?
xtictio ovat # atu v. w hut
aiat a tit. og – if you pa – to u.
        pa, quit aou th co of utouchaiity.
i a ot pa of th ou. may i a wh w a
tuig mooyaic? ov th ttop a huh?
                                you f th athy wi
you a pat of th t-fo a

Notes

p.33, *örtülmüs ürkek özlem:* Turkish, "veiled timid longing".

p.41, *shingles*: the German word is "Gürtelrose", literally: girdle rose. The word "shingles" is derived from the Latin *cingulum* and *cinctura*, a girdle.

p.129, *diver, mangle / (of the fourfold sense of scripture):* According to the German critic Michael Braun, Draesner has referred in connection with this poem to a sermon by the medieval mystic Meister Eckart who described the unfathomability of the Holy Scriptures as comparable with a bottomless ocean. The "fourfold sense of scripture" refers to the mystical dimensions of Scripture, which, beginning with the literal, proceed through three further mystical levels: allegorical, tropological and anagogical.

p.147, *revontulet*: the Finnish word for the Northern Lights, literally: fox's fires.

p.151, *synger med fuld styrke*: Danish, "singing with all their might". According to Ulrike Draesner, a Danish local newspaper with this heading was found in the letterbox of the house in Svendborg where Bertolt Brecht had spent most of the 1930s in exile. The article was referring to crickets.

p.173, *founding of linguistics*: on 2nd February 1788 Sir William Jones, a judge at the Supreme Court of Judicature in Bengal, held a lecture at the then-named Asiatick Society of Calcutta in which he proposed the existence of a Indo-European family of languages (including Latin, Greek, Celtic, Persian and Sanskrit) descended from a common, albeit extinct source, which became known as Proto-Indo European.

p.193, *mire snite* (mud snipe): an English dialect word for the common snipe, *Gallinago gallinago*. The name used in the German poem, *rüsken-snepp*, is a German local name for the same bird, which, like mire-snite references its habitat, literally: rushes snipe.

p.220, *exit erdbeer-klee*: a video of the poem, developed by the author with Stefan Harder for the Berlin Haus für Poesie's 2020 Poetry Festival, can be viewed at https://www.youtube.com/watch?v=8zdovV_cko4

Biographies

Ulrike Draesner was born in Munich in 1962. She studied English Literature, Philosophy and German Literature in Munich, where she completed a Ph.D. on the medieval romance *Parzival* in 1992, and at Oxford, where she returned as a visiting fellow from 2015–17. She is one of the most distinguished poets writing in German today, and has also translated work by, among others, Gertrude Stein, Michèle Métail and H.D., as well as Louise Glück's volumes *Averno* (2007) and *Wild Iris* (2008). Draesner's eight volumes of poetry include her debut *gedächtnis-schleifen* (*memory loops*, 1995) as well as *für die nacht geheuerte zellen* (*cells hired for the night*, 2001), *kugelblitz* (*ball lightning*, 2005), *subsong* (*subsong*, 2014) and her long poem *doggerland* (2021). She has written seven novels, the most recent of which are *Sieben Sprünge vom Rand der Welt* (*Seven Leaps from the Edge of the World*, 2014), which was shortlisted for the German Book Prize and in which a chorus of characters tell of forced migration in Middle and Eastern Europe between 1939 and the present day, *Kanalschwimmer* (*Channel Swimmer*, 2019), and *Schwitters* (2020), which follows the artist Kurt Schwitters into exile (1937–1948) from Hanover via Norway and London until his death in the Lake District. She has also published three books of stories and five volumes of essays and lectures. Among many other awards for her poetry and fiction, she received the Grand Prize of the German Literary Fund in 2021 for her life's work. She lives in Berlin and Leipzig, where she is a professor of Creative Writing at the German Literature Institute.

Iain Galbraith, born in 1956 in the West of Scotland, studied German, French and Comparative Literature in Cambridge, Freiburg and Mainz, where he taught English for ten years. His recent publications include a volume of poems, *The True Height of the Ear* (Arc, 2018), as well as translations of W.G. Sebald's *Across the Land and the Water. Selected Poems* (Penguin, 2012), Esther Dischereit's *Sometimes a Single Leaf. Selected Poems* (Arc, 2020) and Reinhard Jirgl's novel *The Unfinished* (Seagull, 2020). He has edited five anthologies of poetry and is also a translator into German, including plays by Enda Walsh and Che Walker and volumes of poetry by Alice Oswald and John Burnside. Since 2019 he has contributed monthly essays to the online platform *openDemocracy* on subjects as diverse as data centres, Edgar Reitz's film series *Heimat*, and personal poultry in London's City. He has won a number of prizes for his work, including the Stephen Spender Prize (2014), the Popescu Prize for European Poetry Translation (2015), the Schlegel-Tieck Prize in 2016 for his translation of Jan Wagner's *Self-portrait with a Swarm of Bees. Selected Poems* (Arc) and again in 2019 for a translation of Esther Kinsky's novel *River* (Fitzcarraldo). He lives in Wiesbaden, Germany.

www.ingramcontent.com/pod-product-compliance
Lightning Source LLC
Chambersburg PA
CBHW022006160426
43197CB00007B/304
* 9 7 8 1 8 4 8 6 1 7 8 5 8 *